Stringhalt

Runs with the Lanarkshire and Renfrewshire Fox-Hounds

And Other Sporting Incidents

Stringhalt

Runs with the Lanarkshire and Renfrewshire Fox-Hounds
And Other Sporting Incidents

ISBN/EAN: 9783744746144

Printed in Europe, USA, Canada, Australia, Japan

Cover: Foto ©Andreas Hilbeck / pixelio.de

More available books at **www.hansebooks.com**

RUNS

WITH THE

LANARKSHIRE & RENFREWSHIRE

FOX-HOUNDS,

AND OTHER SPORTING INCIDENTS.

BY

"STRINGHALT."

GLASGOW:

KERR & RICHARDSON, 89 QUEEN STREET.

1874.

PREFACE.

AT the request of a number of gentlemen who hunt with the Lanarkshire and Renfrewshire Fox-Hounds, I have thrown together a few sporting reminiscences connected with this particular district, and at the same time have added reports of a number of runs which I have from time to time written for the *Glasgow Herald* and *Sporting Gazette*. I regret that I have not retained the dates of some of them; but most men who have hunted with these hounds will remember the events.

ORIGIN

GLASGOW HOUNDS.

The first record I can find connected with hounds in Lanarkshire is an account of a meeting held at Bothwell Bridge, on the 8th April, 1771, when it was agreed as follows, by John Orr, Esq., Barrowfield, on the one part, and John Baird and Robert Dunmore, Esqs. (as taking burden on them for the Glasgow Hunt), on the other part:—

That they shall have a united Hunt, which shall be called by the name of "The Roberton Hunt," and which shall have two meetings at this place annually. The first of these to be some time in October or November next, as the gentlemen shall agree upon; and the second (or Spring Meeting) to be in April following.

The following regulations are now agreed upon, to which such others as are afterwards thought proper shall be added:—

1st. That a Preses shall be chosen at every April Meeting, before the Hunt party, who shall continue for a year, and shall have the regulation of everything concerning the Hunt for that year; and Captain Roberton is accordingly chosen for the first two meetings.

2ndly. That a Treasurer shall be chosen annually, into whose hands each member of the Hunt shall pay, the first day of the meeting, such sums as shall be thought necessary for paying any incidental expenses, of stopping earth, damages done to enclosures, &c., &c.; and Mr. Matthew Orr, Stobcross, is accordingly chosen for the first two meetings.

3rd. That the Hunt shall have a uniform, to be worn by all the members at these meetings; and it is agreed that the uniform shall be a dark brown frock, of Hunters' beaver, made without lapells, and to button at the sleeves; with a waistcoat of the same cloth, with lapells, and lined with white silk shag; both to have plain silver buttons.

4th. That the Hunt shall have an Earth-stopper, and they shall give him annually a coat and waistcoat of coarse green cloth, and two pair of white plaiding breeches, and a leather cap; and they nominate for that office Thomas Greer, being satisfied that he is properly qualified for that important charge.

5th. Whereas, it will be necessary to have a Kennel Yard and Benches put up for the Hounds, Captain Roberton has been so good as promise to supply the Hunt with Benches, and wood to make the Kennel Yard of, for the putting up of which the Hunt are to be at the expense.

SECOND MEETING.

BOTHWELL BRIDGE,
22nd August, 1771.

At a Meeting of the Roberton Hunt, Members present—

CAPTAIN ROBERTON, PRESES.
MESSRS. GEORGE BUCHANAN.
ANDREW LEITCH.
MATTHEW ORR.

Resolved, that the Kennel Yard shall be built as agreed upon at the last Spring Meeting, and James Wilson was engaged to execute the same.

THIRD MEETING.

At a Meeting of the Roberton Hunt, Members present—

CAPTAIN ROBERTON, PRESES.
MESSRS. JOHN BAIRD.
JOHN BOGLE.
ARCHIBALD BOGLE.
ALLAN SCOTT, Cowlairs.
ANDREW HOUSTON.
ANDREW LEITCH.
ROBERT DUNMORE.
JOHN ORR, Barrowfield.
ROBERT DREGHORN.
CAPTAIN STEWART.
MATTHEW ORR.

Absent Members:—

SIR THOMAS WALLACE.
MESSRS. THOMAS HOUSTON.
GEORGE BUCHANAN
THOMAS DONALD.
JOHN STUART.
JAMES DUNLOP, Carmile.
JAMES DUNLOP, Houshill.
ROBERT MUIRHEAD.
CAPTAIN NAPIER.
BRUCE CAMPBELL.
WILLIAM BOGLE.

The above list of gentlemen are the constituted Members of the "Roberton Hunt," and it is resolved that no more Members are to be admitted without being Ballotted for, at a Meeting of the Hunt, nine of whom make a quorum, and a majority of white balls admit.

Resolved, That each of the Members shall pay a Guinea to the Treasurer, to defray contingent expenses.

Resolved, That Thomas Greer, the Earth-stopper, shall be furnished with a green coat and waistcoat, two pair of plaiding breeches, the coat to have a red cape, and to have "Earth-stopper to the Roberton Hunt" embroidered on the breast of it.

Resolved, That it shall be left to the Preses and Treasurer to give orders about stalling the stables and putting up the Kennel Yard.

Resolved, That there shall be a board made of an oval form to enlarge the table; that it shall be one foot wider, and four feet longer, than the present one—this to be left to the Preses and Secretary.

Resolved, That the Treasurer shall bespeak four Delph bowls to make a bottle of Rum each, with "The Roberton Hunt" written on them.

It is ordered, That the Treasurer shall send up a hogshead of London porter, six dozen strong Beer, five dozen Port wine, and one dozen Sherry.

It is also ordered, That the Treasurer shall send up six or eight gallons French Brandy, put into a Dutch case.

Resolved, That the first "Hunting Meeting" shall begin on the first Glasgow Fast-day, and that the "Glasgow Hounds" shall hunt that day at Blantyre Whins, Mr. Orr's hounds being to hunt the day following at Orbiston.

It is ordered that the Treasurer shall send up forty stone of cracklings before the Meeting.

It is recommended to the Preses to order Greer, and other people, to have a strict search for all the earths in the country before the Meeting.

Resolved, That all the Members of the Hunt shall be obliged to take off the uniform from Mr. James Hamilton before the first Meeting, and that no Member shall go to the field during the Meeting without it, under a penalty of paying one guinea for each offence.

It is desired that Alex. Gray shall each day during the Meeting have a dinner provided at thirty shillings—each of the gentlemen present to pay two shillings. If the number does not amount to fifteen, the difference to be made up to Gray by the Treasurer; and if they exceed that number, the money to be disposed of as the Members shall think proper.

FIRST HUNTING MEETING.

Thursday, 14th November, 1771.

"GLASGOW HOUNDS."

Members in the Field—

CAPTAIN ROBERTON.
JOHN ORR.
ALLAN SCOTT, Cowlairs.
CAPTAIN NAPIER.
MATTHEW ORR.
GEORGE HOUSTON, Visiting Member.

Found a Fox at Hamilton Moor, and killed him above ground. Hunted Hare afterwards. Indifferent day.

It is difficult to obtain any records of fox-hunting in this neighbourhood up to a recent date. The country has been hunted by Mr. Oswald, Capt. Tait, Sir David Baird, and the Earl of Glasgow, but there are no records of what sport they had. Sometimes the country was divided, and both Renfrewshire and Ayrshire hunted at the same time. Sir D. Baird was a first-rate man across country, and a keen sportsman. Many good runs have taken place in my own recollection within the last twenty-five years, and many good and true sportsmen have been taken away to the happy hunting grounds, whom we will never see again on this side of Jordan. Nimrod, in his "Northern Hunting Tour," tells us of a run with Lord Kelburn long before my day. They found their fox in Hawkhead (in those days a stronghold for breeding) took him straight over the hill at Gleniffer, on to Crofthead, and killed. His Lordship got into a river in the run and had a severe ducking, but got on again, and was up at the finish. I have failed to discover what burn this could have been, unless somewhere in the hollow, before going up the hill. His Lordship had not the best of tempers, and on one occasion when his first whip displeased him, at Langside, he rode at him, and Jack Harris jumped a mill lade to get out of his way. The place was shown for a long time, but modern improvements have, I think, done away with it. Old Kemp talks of a run which took place about this time from Netherton braes, away through Calderwood and Earnock to Avon banks, where they picked up their fox on the rocks dead. Of course, in those days the country was not so woody as it is now, but this must have been a slow hunting run. The first run I had the pleasure of participating in with these hounds was, I think, in 1850, over some of the same country, but nothing like the length. We found on Netherton braes, ran through Castlemilk, on down to Limekilns, and killed just as he was going into Torrance. This was a capital run, as at that time there was no wire, and all sound going. I was riding an old gray I bought from Mr. Barclay, a capital hand at refusing when he was not in " the humour," but on this occasion, more by good luck than anything else, I got up first, and saw the fox killed, passing Mr. C. T. Couper leading his pony up the last hill, one of the best ponies I ever saw, but this run was rather too much for him. I did not like to claim the brush, being then a younker. The next two up were Mr. W. Campbell, and Mr. Clark (house-factor, a veteran sportsman), and an amusing scene now occurred. They both jumped off their horses and claimed the brush, rather an angry altercation taking place. Colonel Buchanan, who was riding his celebrated steeple-chase horse, Alfred, but who had come to grief in a boggy ditch, now got up and gave the brush to Clark. I think he was riding the celebrated little horse Reindeer. What a change there is now in this part of the country. In former days we used to have capital sport here, but now you can't ride a yard for wire. Old Mr. Forbes of Callander came through sometimes to the Meet at Cart Bridge, where it used to be in those days; a rare good un he was to go on a horse Mr. Robert Armour afterwards bought, and which he christened " Forby." On another occasion, poor George Hope Johnston (as good a fellow as ever lived, but the pace was too fast for him at the finish), and

Osy Stewart came through from Dumfriesshire, to try and
"cut us all down, and hang us up to dry," but the ground
was too heavy for George, and I think, at the finish of the
day's work, they had only "two legs" between them to ride
home. A curious incident happened once to a horse belonging
to that prince of sportsmen, Mr. George Middleton. The
hounds met at Milliken Park. Mr. M. was riding a great
long-legged brute that went by the name of the "Camel-
Leopard," and in drawing a strip at Glentyan, when we got
to the top there was no way out the field, having to go back
and lead down, or drop into the road. The Camel got loose,
and running up to the end of the wood, jumped down a drop
of about twenty feet into the road, and, to the astonishment
of everybody, lit on his feet. The Camel could go when he
liked, though, as afterwards, on a bye day, when very few
were out, Mr. M. got away well from the covert, jumped a
tremendous high wall at the top, and had the hounds all to
himself away nearly to the Misty Law, where both fox and
hounds were lost.

Mr. George Middleton was Secretary to the Hunt, and also
to the R.N. Yacht Club, for many years. He was a thorough
all-round sportsman, and good at almost everything. Alas!
poor George! with his merry laugh and fund of wit, and who
always kept us in a roar when going down to the Meet, is no
more, but he has left two chips of the old block, who fully
sustain his "prestige." One of the sharpest things about this
time the L. and R. ever had was over the Fereneze hills.
While the field were coffee-housing, a fox jumped up on the
moor near the Game wood, just before the hounds, and only
about four or five who were near got away on any terms with
them. They raced him down to Johnstone Castle without a
check to ground. John Harrison, or the old "stone wall
jumper," Mr. John Orr on his chestnut, Zezimus, Mr. D.
Hunter on his old mare, and your humble servant on Game-
cock, were the only ones that had the luck to get away, but
we were stumped at a high stone wall at Bardrain. There is
now an accommodating gate in this wall. A very long run

also took place from Linwood Moss—it was a frightfully wet day—when a fox broke in the direction of Houston, and on through Elphinston. The field here, somehow, all got thrown out, and Mr. Thomas Speirs on his stallion was the only one who went on, with two couple of hounds, to ground at Knockmountain. A short sharp spin from Craigmarlock down to Finlaystone originated the Craigmarlock Club, Mr. Allan Scott and Mr. Aird being the chief promoters. Amongst the Members were Messrs. Scott, J. Morrison, R. Armour, D. Hunter, W. Redfern, Aird, Brodie, Murray, Clapperton, C. T. Dunlop, Kelly, &c. Many jovial Meetings we used to have, which were held in the Waverley Hotel, when song and sentiment prevailed to the "wee hour ayont the twal." There was no Forbes Mackenzie in those days. The Club has not held a Meeting for many years. John Harrison, who hunted the hounds before Squires came here, was a first-rate huntsman, but was rather apt to lose his head at an intricate cast with a lot of hard-riding Glasgow men pressing on his hounds (one of whom, a first-rate fellow, and now married, I heard once say, "bother the hounds, can't we do without them"). Latterly, John was a little too much addicted to examining the inside of a black bottle; and I daresay a number of old hunting men will never forget one Christmas day, when, mounted on old Simon, he jumped a tremendous wall, with a wire along the top of it, near the Skiff. John was sent home, and Sandy Chalmers, first whip, took the horn, but they had no sport. The Colonel, when he heard of it, said it served the hunt jolly well right for taking the hounds out on Christmas day. It was entirely a subscription pack then. A nasty accident happened to the father of the present Mr. Sudden, who keeps the excellent hostelry at Kilwinning. One day, when riding a horse belonging to Mr. J. Steven, in jumping out of the Skifflat wood, his horse put his foot in a hole and rolled over him. He was picked up for dead, recovered a little, however, but was never the same man again, and died shortly afterwards. A very unprecedented circumstance once occurred at the Waukmill Glen. A brace of foxes were on foot; one broke on the south side of the covert, with eight couple of hounds, in the direction of Glanderston, and could not be stopped. Harrison, Mr. R. Armour (on Jack Fleming's old horse, Sandy), Mr. J. Barclay, Archy Chalmers, a beginner then (but who has since gone well), and myself, being on that side, went away with them. The rest of the hounds, with the Colonel, were running a fox in the glen. We took our fox on leaving Glanderston and the Pad to the left, over the Kilmarnock road (here Mr. Barclay stopped, having cut his horse), down the boggy hollow, leaving Knockinae to the left on to Uplaw Muir. He then turned and came back very nearly the same line, and we killed him in the open near the farm-house on the north side of the water below the Pad. While we were breaking up our fox, on looking up to the top of the Pad, who should we see but Colonel Buchanan *breaking up* his fox, which he had brought up from Glanderston! the two who'hoops making the welkin ring, and fetching shrill echoes from the hollow earth. This was a very curious incident. We used to have very fair sport in the Carnwath district, when Jack Fleming and the Honourable Mr. Sandilands hunted that part of the county of Lanark with the Linlithgow and Stirlingshire hounds. Both these gentlemen were always very obliging, making handy Meets for the Glasgow division on *certain days* in the year which shall be nameless! Many a good tumbler we have had at old Ritchie's inn before going home. There was also a buxom-looking widow, who kept an hotel there, who received a good deal of attention from the gay lotharios. One run is worth recording, as being the last old Aird ever rode in.

Stonebyres was a favourite Meet, and on this occasion a good fox broke to the south side, and they killed him in the open near Lesmahagow. Just as the hounds were running into their fox, Mr. James Merry and Mr. Aird were riding for the brush, but Aird by a judicious nick was up first, got the brush, and presented it to Willie Wilson, who hunted in those days. When Aird got home he did not feel very well,

B

and remarked that he never perspired during the run. Poor Aird! he took to his bed shortly afterwards, and died of cholera. Aird, although he did not say much, had a great deal of quiet humour about him, and was a great favourite. He had a curious old horse called the "Pig." A story is told of him, *credat judæus*, that in drawing some coverts in the high country above Mains, they came to a wall that was unjumpable, but that Aird got off and gave the Pig "a back," and he got over the field, going round by Shuffler's bottom. I was out that day, but I can't say I saw the occurrence. A portrait of Mr. Aird, painted by subscription, and presented to him, hangs in the smoking-room at Kilmardinny, the residence of R. Dalglish, Esq., who was always a great friend of his. A likeness of the "Pig" also hangs not very far off the old man. Peace be to his "manes."

Mr. Pollock of Broom kept a pack of harriers in the Mearns country for some time. He had some very fair sport. Mr. George Stoddart being one of the best men with them, he was very fond of making young uns, and many a cropper he got. When Mr. Pollock went to Ireland, Mr. John Hamilton of Greenbank took the hounds over, but owing to the great increase of wire, he was obliged to give up the country. I must not forget to mention that when Lord Eglinton hunted the country during the interregnum, when the Colonel went up to Lanarkshire for a season, he showed some excellent sport. One extraordinary long run he once had. Finding an afternoon fox at Treés gorse, he ran him on to the Brimmer, and killed by moonlight. Another very sharp thing took place from the Shaw wood. Found at once, he pointed as for Gleniffer, went very near to Glenfield, but turning to the left, along the face of the hills, went up past the Quarry, where a good many of them were leading, away over a fine grass country to the Game wood, going through which, he then bent away up to the Duchielaw, and down to Graham's gorse, round the face of the hill, nearly to Crofthead, where, as it was getting dark, his Lordship whipped off. In this run Mr. Taylor, "champion comique," killed his celebrated trotting pony by overriding it, not being accustomed to this sort of thing, and had a narrow escape from being prosecuted by the "Society for the Prevention of Cruelty to Animals."

There are a number of sporting events which have occurred in connection with the L. and R. Hunt and its members I think, in 1859, Mr. J. Houldsworth made a bet that he would jump four of his horses over a five foot stone wall. The place chosen was a wall on the Knapps muir, and Harrison had the hounds out on purpose to encourage the horses. Harrison rode the **"Return,"** and cleared it splendidly. Mr. Ryan (now **Mr. H., trainer** at Newmarket) next went at it on the "Niger," but hit it with his hind feet, and had another try, but refused twice. Each horse had three trials. Ryan then mounted "Frenzie." He hit it the first time slightly, the next time he dropped his hind legs, and went bang through the wall, cutting himself badly. "Perfection" now had to try; he hit the wall with his **knees;** the second trial he refused; **but** the last time, Mr. Thyne giving **him a** lead, he cleared it in splendid style (Ryan up). As the match was 4 to win, and 2 to half, it was a draw.

A good many private steeple-chases used **to take place in** former days. A match came off at Houston between Mr. Morrison's "Ballinasloe," and Dr. Grey's "Lucy Long," owners up, when Mr. Morrison won. Another cross country event was run at Kilmarnock, between Mr. Lumsden's "Trotty Veck" and "Ballinasloe." In this instance "Trotty" won, "Lucy Long" third. A steeple-chase **also** took place over a stiff bit of country at the Mearns muir, between Mr. Wm. Campbell's chestnut and a horse belonging to Mr. Thorburn. Mr. A. Clapperton laid off the ground. We had a bit of fun one New-Year's-Day at Carmunnock, when a number of the right sort assembled **to** witness **a** race between **Mr.** Allan Scott's long-legged bay, with Mr. **William Alston up, and Mr.** James Morrison's short-legged bay, **owner up. The** betting was in favour of Mr. Alston, but going the wrong side of a post he had to go back, and **Mr.** Morrison **won easily.** The first steeple I recollect seeing was an "impromptu" affair got up at Kinning Park, near the present Clydesdale Cricket Ground. As far as I can recollect, Reindeer won the chief event, with Bob Thyne up (a first-rate man in his day). Reindeer afterwards won some matches at Houston against a roan horse, ridden by Noble. I recollect going down one day, expecting to see a match between Binks the Bagman and old Isaac (his first appearance in Scotland). Binks failed to appear, and Isaac cantered round the course. Talking of Isaac, I recollect one day at Bogside Meeting (when the late Lord Eglinton was alive), in a steeple-chase refusing the brook, and actually had to be backed into it! but got out and won the race—ridden by Jack Hunter—beating a good horse, Hero, ridden by Colonel Campbell. This Meeting was given up on the death of the late Lady Eglinton, but has since been revived by the present popular Earl. There used to be some good fun at Kilmarnock steeple-chases. As there was no railway in those days, we always drove down, sending on fresh horses to King's Wells, where very often a sporting event came off, early in the morning (which shall be nameless), attended by *not* the *élite* of society. Mr. Hew Young had a very good horse, called the "Dentist," which won several races; Mr. Maxwell, also, won with the "Doctor," and Mr. Norman Buchanan with "Escape." Many a jolly drive we had up and down, but most of the genuine good souls that were wont to join us are now dead or scattered over the world, and Kilmarnock steeple-chases are now no more.

A funny event happened one day, just after the horses had crossed the brook. The late Sandy Fletcher tried to jump it, went in a header, and had to drive home soaked through. In those hardy days one did not care for a wetting, and a story is told of a well-known old Glasgow sportsman, that after dancing all night he came home, changed his clothes, went down to Kilmarnock to hunt with Tait's harriers, had a header in the Pow burn, dined at Kilmarnock, and drove back to Glasgow without changing. Times have changed for the better since then, but I am afraid our hunting *jeunesse dorée* are not so hardy as their forefathers were, although I could name some very promising young uns coming on, chips of the old block. In 1856 that genuine sportsman, Mr. James Hunter of Newmains and Glenapp, suggested that we should have a hunt steeple-chase, gentlemen riders, only horses regularly hunted with the L. and R. hounds to be allowed to run, and riders to wear red coats. · The first race came off at Newmains, for a cup given by Mr. Hunter. Mr. Couper's brown gelding, "Wellington," was made favourite, but he came to grief at the second fence, and "Coltness," belonging to Mr. Hunter, which he bought from Mr. W. Houldsworth, won easy, piloted by "Willie Redfern." Mr. H. afterwards sold this horse to Mr. Little Gilmour, of Leicestershire renown, where he afterwards broke his back. I recollect getting a tremendous cropper in this race, riding a bay of Mr. H.'s. Next year the race was run at Carnwath, when Mr. J. Houldsworth, on his mare "Brunette," won, myself second, on "Lanark." During the race Mr. Couper was again unfortunate. Cannoning with another gentleman at a bank, he got very badly cut in the face. Mr. C. Higginbotham, on his grey, came out at the finish, and looked very like winning, but rolled over in the last field, and was out of it. Next time it was resolved to change the *venue* to the old ground at Houston, where, for the first time, we had 12 and 13 stone steeple-chases for *love*, with a scurry for outside horses added.

These steeple-chases became very popular afterwards amongst all classes of men, and were generally called the "Glasgow Derby," and it was quite a sight to see the road on the way, every sort of vehicle being put into requisition. Mr. J. Houldsworth, Mr. Couper, and Mr. Hinshaw, were the chief winners. The races, which were a first-rate day's outing for all Glasgow, might have been carried on yet if it had not been for the influence of a certain clergyman, persuading the farmers that racing was immoral. Under this uncalled-for interference, the best part of our country was refused us, and a very bad line had to be laid out, the consequence being that at a nasty fence poor Mr. Taylor from Ayrshire was killed. There have been no steeple-chases since this sad event. Bogside races and steeple-chases are, however, now one of the best Meetings in Great Britain, and are increasing in popularity every year, under the patronage of that first-rate sportsman, the Earl of Eglinton, ably assisted in the management of the Meeting by Mr. Shaw of Ayr, the clerk of the course.

Mr. Colin Dunlop some years ago kept a capital pack of harriers, and Chalmers, who for a long time was first whip to the L. and R., hunted them. Under the able management of the Master we had excellent sport. One run in particular, with an outlying roe-deer, over a capital bit of country above Mains, was a clipper. Another good thing we had over Earnock muir. Mr. Dunlop used to go well on a cobby chestnut he bought from Mr. Thorburn, and he was never far off his beauties. Wire stopped his hunting at last. An amusing story is told of an old sportsman having lost the fox hounds in a fog, came up with Mr. Pollock's harriers, which were out that day, and had an excellent spin. A tremendous leap was taken by Mr. John Orr on the "Priest," one day at Netherton braes. Instead of going down through a large grip at the end of the strip, he cleared the whole thing, about 27 feet. Mr. Thorburn, one day at Greenside, stumped the field at a very nasty place on the side of the muir. A dinner of the two hunts, Lanarkshire and Renfrewshire, and Linlithgow and Stirlingshire, took place in the Western Club, Glasgow, in 1850—Jack Fleming in the chair; James Merry, croupier. Fleming and Inglis of Torsonce (a thorough sportsman), were the only gentlemen who wore the dress uniform of their hunt, our local pack not having such a thing. Few casualties have happened in my recollection with these hounds, with the exception of Mr. A. Clapperton and Mr. A. Crum, both of whom broke a leg. Mr. Monteath and Captain Hay Newton, each broke an arm. An excellent picture of the hunt hangs in the lobby of the Western Club, Glasgow, presented to the Club by the late Mr. Hamilton of Minnard, with portraits of most of the old Members in Lord Glasgow's day; and by the kind permission of the managers, I annex a copy of it. The

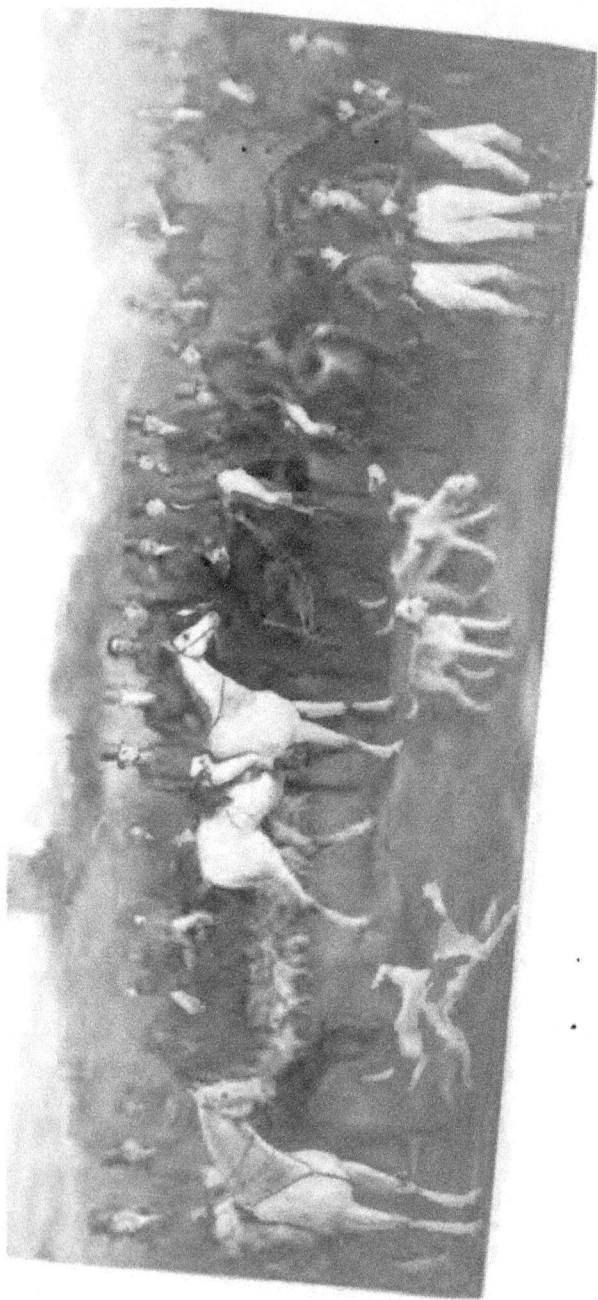

scene is laid at Crookston, and amongst the prominent portraits are Lord Glasgow on the gray horse, Messrs. J. Oswald, S. Dalglish, J. Tennant, George Stirling, George Houston, M. Pearce, W. Houston, R. D. Napier, A. Smith (Jordanhill), Bogle, C. Stirling, Thompson, Chas. Tennant, Sylvester Stirling, and a man, Lochead, who ran after the hounds. Very few of the above are now to the fore, but they were all good men in their day, when the present steeple-chase style of hunting was not in vogue, and no "steam-horses" to take you to the Meet. After them, amongst the most prominent Members were—

SIR M. SHAW STEWART.
MESSRS. T. D. SPEIRS.
JAMES MERRY.
W. AIRD.
GEORGE MIDDLETON.
GEORGE LUMSDEN.
PERSTON.
W. REDFERN.
ALEXANDER CLAPPERTON.
JOHN ORR.
ROBERT ARMOUR.
C. T. DUNLOP.
C. T. COUPER.
W. KELLY.
A. SCOTT.
L. MACBEAN.
JOHN BRODIE.
JOHN S. MILLS.
J. MORRISON.
R. MONTEITH.
GEORGE ALSTON.
W. ALSTON.
J. K. BROWN.
ROBERT PATERSON.
J. MURRAY.
F. MURRAY.
C. HIGGINBOTHAM.
J. HOULDSWORTH.
JOHN HAMILTON (North Park).
JOHN HAMILTON (Greenbank).
JAMES HUNTER (Newmains).
MAJOR HAMILTON (Dalziel).

Messrs. GEORGE POLLOCK (Rhindmuir).
F. R. REID.
GEORGE STODDART.
JOHN BARCLAY.

The following is a List of Subscribers to the Covert Fund of the Lanarkshire and Renfrewshire Fox-Hounds, for Season 1872-73:—

J. H. HOULDSWORTH, Glasgow.
JOHN MONTEITH,   do.
ALEX. CLAPPERTON,   do.
RICHARD KIDSTON,   do.
DONALD MATHESON,   do.
ALLAN SCOTT,   do.
HUGH NEILSON,   do.
C. T. COUPER,   do.
JOHN ORR,   do.
J. H. BALLANTYNE, Greenock.
JOHN DONALDSON, Glasgow.
HENRY LEE HARVEY, Lochwinnoch.
ALEXANDER CRUM, Glasgow.
JOHN HAMILTON, of Greenbank, Mearns.
ADAM MORRISON, Glasgow.
J. D. HAMILTON,   do.
GEORGE J. KIDSTON, do.
THOMAS JACKSON, Coatbridge.
JAMES COATS, Glasgow.
DURHAM KIPPEN, Glasgow.
MATTHEW ROBERTSON, Foxbar, Paisley.
JOHN WATSON, Govan Foundry, Govan.
WILLIAM JAMES FINLAYSON, Johnstone.
JOHN C. PEARSON, Glasgow.
GEORGE J. SMITH,   do.
A. C. HOLMS,   do.
COLIN R. DUNLOP,   do.
ALEX. COCHRAN,   do.
THOMAS R. CAMERON, Paisley.
JAMES GEORGE DUNLOP, Glasgow.
M. T. FOZIER,   do.
ANDREW HUNTER,   do.
JAMES SELKIRK,   do.
JAMES COUPER,   do.
GEORGE COATS, Paisley.
EDWARD COLLINS, Jun., Glasgow.
C. J. CUNNINGHAME, of Craigends.

WILLIAM FAULDS, Oakshawhill, Paisley.
MATTHEW ARTHUR, Glasgow.
JAMES WALLACE,   do.
F. W. PERMAN,   do.
ROBERT MONTEITH,   do.
JOHN BUCHANAN, Glasgow.
JASPER HOWAT,   do.
DANIEL M'FARLANE,   do.
JOHN S. WILSON,   do.
J. GARDNER MUIR,   do.
F. R. REID,   do.
WILLIAM CAMPBELL,   do.
ALEXANDER RONALDSON, Jun., Glasgow.
GEORGE D. FISHER,   do.
ALEXANDER CROSS, Jun.,   do.
ROBERT ROBSON,   do.
DUNCAN HOYLE GIBB, Greenock.
SIR M. R. S. STEWART, Bart., Ardgowan.
JOHN JAMES POLLOCK, Glasgow.
GEORGE W. RICHARDSON, Paisley.
NEALE THOMSON, Camphill.
D. H. M'DOWAL, Garthland, Lochwinnoch.
WILLIAM WILSON, Glasgow.
PETER WHITE, Jun., do.
GEORGE RONALDSON, Linwood.
JOHN A. BRODIE, Glasgow.
HENRY FERGUSON, do.

In 1872, Mr. George Jardine of Hallside was just beginning to come out as a first-rate sportsman, and being well mounted, was going into hunting with a keenness which I have hardly ever seen equalled. Unfortunately, to the extreme regret of all true hunting men, with whom Mr. Jardine was a great favourite, through an unfortunate accident he lost one of his legs, and was obliged to give up riding. However, he still encourages sport of all kinds, keep a good steeple-chaser or two, and often comes out on wheels, always having a good supply of refreshment on board for any drouthy fox-hunter. Referring to Mr. Jardine's horses, he had a rare good one called the "General," and one day James Sudden cut down all the Ayrshire men with him. Unfortunately, the "General," who looked very like winning a big thing some day, broke his leg at Bogside, while going well, and had to be destroyed. I may mention that amongst those who are not subscribers, young Mr. Cockburn, veterinary surgeon, and Mr. James Sudden, landlord of the Eglinton Arms, Kilwinning, are first-rate men with hounds.

At the present time (January,1874) the Colonel hardly ever goes up to Lanarkshire, except for cub-hunting, the country being not worth hunting on account of woods and wire. I have seen, however, some very fair runs in the New Monkland country, and also at Castlemilk, but the last-named country is now almost unrideable on account of wire.

Renfrewshire, I am happy to say, never showed more foxes than at the present time. Most of the best part of the country is in the hands of Colonel Buchanan, our esteemed Master, and Mr. C. J. Cunninghame of Craigends, a keen sportsman, quite enough guarantee for the preservation of foxes. I must not forget to give a word of praise to old Scott, the keeper at Barrochan, who *always* has a fox; in fact, it has become quite a proverb in the Hunt, " We're sure to find a Barrochan." Captain Stewart of Castlemilk has always no end of foxes; and old Hunter can always show both game and plenty of the " varmint." The best Meets are Houston kennels, Finlayston, Bishopton, Bridge of Weir, Broadfield, Neilston (for the Pad), and the Fereneze hills. Mr. George Kidston, a genuine sportsman, and keen preserver of foxes, has taken a long lease of Finlayston house and shootings, one of Colonel Buchanan's properties, lying in the centre of the best part of the country, and, it is needless to say, there is a fox in every covert.

Squires, who succeeded John Harrison, is as fresh as ever, and generally manages to kill his fox, and his cheery voice has lost none of its music.

Through the kindness of an old Member of the Hunt, I am enabled to give the following quotations from his diary :—

" October 20th, 1849.—Met at Craigends Gate to open the season—a large Meet. Trotted on to Barlogan. Found at once, and ran a sharp ring of a couple of miles over the muir, and back to covert. Two very unfortunate accidents happened in this spin. Mr. George Baird's horse, after clearing a wall, took paralysis, and had to be shot; and another gentleman broke his mare's leg sharp off, and the mare was also destroyed. After ringing about, got our fox away again, but unfortunately ran to ground. Found again in Elphinstone, and had ten miles at a clipping pace, very few up at the finish. Mr. Barclay riding a new chestnut, cut him very badly, and had to drive home.

"Saturday, October 27th.—Bridge of Weir. Drove down 'Tom Thumb.' A nasty morning, misty and rain, which, however, took off about one o'clock. Found in the Torr Wood, and got him away towards Castle Semple, but he turned back, and we ran through Carruth to Duchal, where the drains, as usual, saved his life. Mr. James Merry, who was then acting M. F. H., tumbled into a brook during the run, and sundry other spills took place. 'Jerry' badly cut.

"Nov. 3.—Castle Semple. 'Harlequin' not fit, but George Wilkie offered me a mount on his chestnut, but no persuasion could get him into a horse-box. Willie Campbell, however, offered me his old game horse, which he had ridden down to the station, he intending to ride Mr. M'Kenzie's gray, and I was admirably carried for the day. Found a leash of foxes in Greenside; all three broke in view of the hounds, ran one to Carruth again, as usual, into a drain. Went back, got on the line of another one, and went a burster down to Castle Semple, where, owing to dead leaves, scent failed, drew the Scifflat blank.

"Nov. 10th.—Met at Neilston village. Drew the Pad and Knockinae blank, but found at Fereneze, and ran as straight as an arrow to Johnstone Castle, and killed. Pace tremendous, the best of the season, many casualties, and Mr. J. Mills' horse had to be left at Johnstone. Rode a new purchase from Hew Young, the 'Screw,' and was well carried.

"Nov. 17th.—Johnstone Castle. Drew the coverts here and Gleniffer blank. Found at Hawkhead, had a pumper up to Gleniffer, and back to Hawkhead — time, twenty-five minutes.

"Nov. 24th.—Bishopton. A good run, but did not kill.

"Nov. 27th.—Cathcart Bridge.. A large field out, and a great number of people on foot. **Found** at Merrylees, and killed. Found again at the Lynn, and had **the** run of the season, one hour and ten minutes, and killed in **the open.**

"Dec. 22.—Hillend (Lanarkshire). Only **four** men out, the two Messrs. Wilkie, Willie Campbell, and myself. Found at once in Auchengray, and ran straight to Armadale over a boggy country. The scent being breast high, we fell behind, and had **to be** guided by "chawbacons." Caught them up near Avon bridge, where the fox doubled, and we lost him— time $1\frac{1}{2}$ hours. Had to ride home 25 miles. All the subscribers annoyed they were not out.

"Feb. 9th, 1850.—Met after a long frost at Bridge of Weir. Drew the Torr, Carruth, Milliken, and Castle Semple, **all** blank, and gave it up.

"16th February, 1850.—Went through with Redfern, Jamieson, Kelly, and John Orr, to meet Ramsay at Cathlaw, east gate (Linlithgowshire). Found plenty of foxes, and had a fast half-hour over a heavy country. Kelly's horse badly cut.

"Feby. 23rd.—Bishopton. Found at Westferry, and ran a very fast ring of about nine miles to ground; found again in Elphinstone, and had a splitter of one hour twenty minutes to ground at Finlayston, only nine men up, lots of horses having come to grief; two left at Port-Glasgow, one at Paisley, and one at Govan.

"Tuesday, 8th Oct.—The Kennels, and had a good run.

"Saturday, 13th Oct.—Castle Semple, and a short spin from Linwood to Milliken.

"26th October.—Shelford Toll. A good run from **Caldwell** to the Brimmer to ground, and a fast hour and a half from the Pad, and had to whip off at dark.

"2nd Nov.—Johnstone Castle, and had a very fine hunting run of half an hour.

"Saturday, 25th January, 1851.—Castle Semple. A very

fine run of forty-five minutes from Bridge of **Weir to Carruth,** and killed. Barclay got the brush.

"**Feb.** 1st.—Bishopton. Found in Westferry, had a sharp **burst and** lost. Found again in Elphinstone, **ran** him through the Wreas over High Barlogan, and back nearly to where they found. A slight check took place here, or nobody would have seen them again. **Picked** it up again, and ran to the Kilmalcolm strips, and **back** over Barscube **hill to Barrochan,** on through Drums to **ground** at Westferry. This was **one of** the longest runs **that has taken place in** this country."

LANARKSHIRE & RENFREWSHIRE FOX-HOUNDS.

CUB-HUNTING.

As a great number **of our readers have a** very imperfect idea what the above term means, **a few** words will **easily** explain it. Fox-hounds, as a rule, will **not take** naturally to hunting the fox only, but at first will dash after any species of game, strange as it may seem to the uninitiated; not like a pointer, who, when quite a puppy, will point naturally even at barn-door fowls **or** any small birds; therefore, the object of cub-hunting is to **train** the young hounds into hunting the fox, and break them off other game, especially roe-deer, the size of whose bodies impregnates the air with a very strong **scent; and unless young hounds** have plenty opportunities of seeing deer, **with a** cold **scent, or a** blank **day, the** best are apt to flash off after *haunch.* **In** olden times it was often the habit of masters of hounds **to begin by** hunting hare, on purpose to make the hounds put their **noses** down and hunt patiently **on a** cold scent, and then take to hunting the fox afterwards. And even now many packs of harriers are composed entirely of what **are** called dwarf fox-hounds. **Before** taking the field, even in cub-hunting, the huntsman is not idle, **having a** great deal of work to do in exercising the young hounds, taking long rides in the country, especially in the direction of the different districts likely to be hunted, not only to get his hounds into condition, but to accustom them to the country, and make them steady on the road. After all these preliminaries are gone through (the difficulties attending which are little known or cared for by the swell in his red coat, who turns out on the opening day to gallop *over* the hounds), the first day's cub-hunting takes place. The date of commencement entirely depends upon the state of the country, being much earlier in England than in Scotland, on account of the crops being sooner off the ground. The hounds are cast into covert early in the morning, while the dew is on the ground. No one is acquainted with the exact spot where the Meet is to take place, unless it be some particular friend, some regular old stager, whose age, or sometimes purse, precludes him from joining in the regular chase, but who, ever passionately fond of the sport, loves to witness the schooling of the young hounds. An early hour is selected, to prevent the attendance of a number of persons, who, by their noise, would distract the attention of the hounds. It is delightful to see the pack thrown into covert at daybreak, when all is freshness and joy around—when the choristers of the wood are in full harmony, and everything appears fresh and beautiful. The whips are placed so as to stop the hounds if an old fox goes away, the object being to kill a cub and blood the young hounds, thus giving them a taste of the animal they are intended to hunt. The huntsman generally takes out some old and steady hounds, who by their example teach the young ones what they are to do; and it is astonishing how a young, well-bred hound will score to the cry of an old steady customer, whose voice is never mistaken by the huntsman. Young foxes at this time of the year are generally easily brought to hand, and a sensible huntsman will allow no hallooing and cracking of whips by his servants, which serves only one purpose, to frighten the young hounds and disgust the old; and, as "Scrutator" says—"I have often heard, when a young hound is running riot, a whipper-in hallooing

with all his might and cracking his whip, and I can conceive
little ' Mischief' safe in high covert chuckling within herself,
and saying, ' All very fine, Mr. Jack, but I don't care a straw
for your cracked voice; I shall have my fun out,'"—the
proper way being to wait till the young rioter comes out,
thinking the coast clear, and then pounce upon her with one
or two good dozes of whip-cord. But now the hounds are
running in full chorus.

> " Not Handel's sweet music more pleases the ear,
>   Than that of the hounds in full cry."
>
> *Somerville.*

A whole litter of cubs is afoot; now "Vanguard" views one,
then "Valiant." "Have a care, 'Vanity,'" cries the whip,
as the little beggar makes a dart at "Pussy." They are
running with a burning scent—

> " Making the welkin answer them,
>   And fetching shrill echoes from the hollow earth;"

and with the animating cheer of old Squires, the blood in the
veins of every true fox-hunter tingles again. "Who-hoop," at
last a cub is killed; a great deal of ceremony now takes place:
in the breaking up of the fox the young hounds are all
collected together, and encouraged by every means to taste
blood, and if any promising young fox-hunter is present, who
has this day seen his first fox killed, he is *blooded* also, and
must submit patiently to having a *pad* drawn across his face.

Colonel Buchanan has begun the season well, finding
plenty of foxes in Lanarkshire, and we hear capital accounts
of Renfrewshire, his crack country. We will defer, however
giving a more detailed account of the hounds, &c., till after
the opening day, which takes place on the 31st October, at
Houston, when we hope to see going in their old places, not
only the tried and keen supporters of the Hunt, but also a
number of new young 'uns sporting the pink.

SPLENDID SPORT WITH THE LANARKSHIRE AND RENFREWSHIRE FOX-HOUNDS.

On account of the unexampled severity of the weather, I am sorry I have not been able to report anything worth recording in the *Herald* of the above celebrated Scotch pack. What with rain and wind, hounds have hardly been able to hunt at all. However, the runs of the following three days amply make up for the previous scarcity of sport:—

Thursday, 7th.—Met at Hawkhead south gate, the Meet having been put off from Tuesday on account of the funeral of Captain Speirs, M.P. for the county, whose death—cut off in the prime of life—is lamented by all classes; a keen sportsman in every sense of the word, a first-rate preserver of foxes, and a popular country gentleman. Squires trotted direct up towards Waukmill Glen, where, in the new gorse, they found at once. He broke to the left up through Patterton round covert, over the Stewarton Road, through the Rouken, passing Eastwood to the left, on to ground in Lady Mary's Wood, trotted back to the Rouken, and came on what Colonel Buchanan thought was a run fox, as the hounds caught him at once. They then made a move up the country to Glanderston Gorse, the shooting around which is leased by the popular Secretary of the Hunt and keen sportsman, Mr. J. Morrison, where, the moment the hounds were thrown in, no less than two brace of foxes were afoot, one of which gave them a good ring round the rocks to ground, near Waukmill Glen.

Saturday, 9th.—Met at Barrochan, where, much to the disappointment of Mr. Hinshaw and his keeper, Scott, the home coverts were drawn blank. This, however, was not to be wondered at, as the *lie* is very bare, and from the stormy state of the weather, the foxes are mostly in the low country, where there is much better covert. There were two litters here, and no doubt exists that Mr. Hinshaw is one of the keenest preservers in the county. Drew the Wreas and Corslie covert blank, but found in Elphinstone big wood. After dusting his jacket well in covert, he broke at the bottom end, going straight through Lawfield Gorse, on up the hill to the left, round High Barlogan, and back to the Wreas; but here, as the country was covered by the *franchise* hollowing on every hill, Squires gave it up, and trotted away down to Drums, where they found at once. He came out at the bottom of the glen, and bent up the hill to the left over the march wall, as if his point was Elphinstone, but turned sharp back again to the right, going over the left side of Barscube Hill, and on to ground at Knockmountain Gorse. This was a very pretty twenty minutes, the hounds going as straight as an arrow from find to finish.

Tuesday, 12th, Caldwell.—Found in a moment (Colonel Mure being a keen preserver of foxes), and went away over the Lugton Road, up the hill towards Dunlop, and back to the left, to ground at the Grange Wood. This was a very pretty twenty-five minutes for hounds, but part of the line was rather boggy, and "'ammer, 'ammer on the 'ard, 'ard road," was the order of the day. Now came the run of the season as yet. The moment the hounds were thrown into Shelford Toll covert, a fine old dog-fox broke near the toll and went away a burster as if for Neilston Pad, but, suddenly changing his mind, turned sharp to the left at Smiddy Hill, down over the Cowdon Burn, across the road and up the hill to Millthird. This was a pumper for the horses, and the hounds got rather the better of them. Colonel Buchanan, having got a bad start, seeing the hounds turning to the left, galloped up the road and caught the hounds at a small strip of wood on the top of the hill, with their heads up. The fox, being pumped with the tremendous pace they had raced him up the hill, had lain down. He jumped up in view of the hounds, and away they went "a-splitter" on to Middleton, through which the fox went—turning to the right down to the old road, then along the face of the hill past Woodneuk, West Arthurlie, and the game covert to the gorse at Trees.

The hounds going through the bottom side had a slight check Mr. J. Orr, Mr. Thorburn, and Mr. Couper having taken the top line, and being well up, viewed two couple of hounds going on out at the west end. One of them rode back and told Squires, who at once cast forward and hit him off over the boggy glen, rather pointing towards the reservoir. They went by Brownside Braes, leaving Glenfield to the right, on to Gleniffer. The fox came out at top end near a row of high trees, and turned down to the right over the road past Staneley Moor, leaving Greenshieldmuir to the right, very near on to Bardrain Wood, as if his point was now Johnstone Castle. Here, being very far through, he began dodging, and turning to the left, lay down before the hounds; but jumping up in view, they raced him into a drain near the Witch Burn, bolted and killed him. Time, one hour and ten minutes; distance gone over, about twelve miles, with only one check. This run was acknowledged by all who were out to be one of the very best these hounds have ever had, being over the cream of the country, all grass and good going. Squires went in his usual form on "Whiteface;" in fact, the old 'un is very hard to beat, always sticking to his hounds, and can show his heels to some of the hard riders yet. He got a nasty bite from the fox when bolting him, which, I am afraid, will prevent him using his right hand for a day or two. I hope to be able, before the season is over, to give you another screed; but it will be a long time, I am afraid, before I shall have the pleasure of chronicling such a run as the above.

LANARKSHIRE & RENFREWSHIRE FOX-HOUNDS.

Since the opening day, when they had such a good thing, our local pack have had nothing particularly worth recording; but to many old hunting men, who now no longer participate in the joys of the chase, an account of what is going on in the pursuit of the noble science, however meagre, is always interesting; and many a good laugh they sometimes have upon the size of the jumps, as related by the young 'uns after dinner, the fences having grown much larger since their hunting days. "Squires" has killed six brace and a half of foxes since he began regular hunting, unfortunately falling in mostly with dodgers, and sometimes the field have been to blame in heading a good 'un when his mind was bent in going away. On Tuesday, the 15th, they had a short thing from the Skiff of about four miles, the only fault being too much "Macadamizing." After running down to the bottom end, his point evidently being Johnstone Castle, he turned up the glen and broke to the west, leaving North Muir Dykes to the left, then down towards Castle-Semple, along the Beltree Strip to ground at Lochside House. The Colonel, Squires, Dr. Wolsey, Mr. Cramsie (5th Fusiliers), Mr. Jackson, and Mr. Clapperton only got away, the rest of the field were left coffee housing at the bottom of the covert, and, I am told, had a Mount Pisgah gallop without hounds, led by a hard-riding member of the Hunt, towards Caldwell. Went back and killed a brace. Another fox broke away up by Bardrain, but even suppose Squires had wanted, the high country was too hard to ride.

Saturday, 18th.—Met at Barrochan, and I need hardly repeat what I have so often said before, wherever old Scott is the "*tod*" is not very far off. While they were drawing the Northend Wood a fox was viewed away from the Garden-Stick covert. It was a little time before Squires got his hounds on, and then, owing to a nasty catching scent, as is generally the case with a lifting frost, they hunted him slowly on past Boghall, over the road to the high wood above Park Erskine Glen. Just as the hounds went away, it would have frightened some of the quiet ones to hear the anathemas of old Fulton, as some of the duffers, who don't know sown grass from the flags in Buchanan Street, went helter-skelter over his seeds. But to return to our *muttons*,—or rather the hounds,—the fox doubled back out at the bottom end, crossed the Drums Road near to Hardgate Toll, and went on—very

pretty but slow hunting—all left to themselves, passing Kirk-
lands on to Barrochan, where they lost him, owing to there
being no scent. It was a treat to see the hounds hunting it
out all in a body, and, as a good judge remarked, the Colonel's
hounds can burst him up with a scent, and hunt him with
none! Found again at once in Corslie Hill gorse, where he
ran a great risk of losing his life, on account of there being
riders in every possible position than the right one. However, as luck would have it, he got away down towards Barrochan. Being headed at the road, he turned back towards
Clives, which covert he did not enter, but went over the cream
of the Renfrewshire country to ground at Elphinstone. A
rather amusing incident occurred during the day.

> " Dismounting, said one, at a gate which was fast,
> The crowd pushing by knocked me down as they passed;
> My horse seized that moment to take his own fling;
> Oh! who'll again doubt hunting a good-natured thing."
>
> *Warburton.*

A rough-and-ready party, from the middle of Renfrewshire,
caught the above gentleman's horse, who at once tipped him
a shilling. "Hoots, man," says he, rejecting the proffered
"bob," "d'ye no ken I'm ane o' your ainsels"—highly in-
dignant at being mistaken for anyone but an A1 man with
the L. and R. pack. On the way home I met with the usual
number of men with plenty of excuses for not being there or
thereabouts; and to quote Warburton again:—

> " How trifling a cause will oft lose us a run,
> From the find to the finish how few see the fun;
> A *mischance* it is called when we come to a halt—
> Did you e'er hear of one who confessed it a fault?"

A DAY'S HAWKING WITH MR. EWEN OF
EWENFIELD.

Falconry, or what in olden times was called hawking, is of
very ancient origin, and has been traced back, as an Eastern

sport, to a period anterior to the Christian era. In Britain it seems to have been followed before the time of the Heptarchy; and in the celebrated Bayeux tapestry Harold is figured with a hawk on his hand. In England, after the Norman Conquest, it made great strides, being much indulged in by kings, nobles, and ladies. In the present day an attempt is being made in several quarters to revive the noble art, and we are informed that in Scotland the Marquess of Bute is taking a strong liking to the sport, being out often with Mr. Ewen, and is now on the look-out for a good falconer. Having received an invitation from Mr. Ewen to have a day's hawking with him, we drove about ten miles out of Ayr, to the high land, where there is a fine open country, as when it is enclosed it does not do for this sport, the birds taking refuge in the fences, thus spoiling the "swoop." Here we met Peter with the hawks. Peter is quite a character—very keen—and Mr. E. tells us he considers him the best falconer he has ever seen. He was falconer to the Duke of Leeds before he came to Mr. Ewen. The peregrine falcon is the one Mr. E. flies, of which he has six, well trained by old Peter, one four-year-old, three two-year-old, and two yearlings. The falconer carries the hawk he is going to fly on his wrist, hooded, and a small strap between his fingers called the "jesses," while a boy goes behind with the cadge, a frame of wood, with four legs, strapped over his shoulders, carrying the rest of the hawks, all of which have small bells tied round their *arms*, with a small piece of leather called the *bewitt*. Mr. E. hawks grouse and partridges. In olden times the heron was the chief object of pursuit, but in these days the scarcity of these birds does not give the falconer any opportunity of training his birds to them. A couple of steady pointers or setters are generally taken out to find the game, and great care is taken not to fly the falcon unless the dogs are quite sure, as when the falcon is disappointed, he is apt to go after other "quarry," and is difficult to lure. But now, Mr. E.'s celebrated red setter is standing, well backed by his black pointer. Peter cautiously goes round, generally up-wind, unhoods the falcon on his wrist, and throws her up. She immediately begins to ascend, going round in circles, until far up in the air, and nothing pleases a keen falconer more than to see his birds rising well, and, from the enormous height they go up, it is wonderful how they can see the "quarry" so near to the ground. Whenever old Peter sees the falcon coming round with his head pointing in the direction where the covey is sitting, he cries out, looking up to his bird, "Hillo! my lass; hooha, ha, ha!" and walking in, flushes the birds to the word, "Gare'oh"—the falcon at once selecting his bird, closes his wings, and swoops down like a cannon-ball, unerringly striking him, always with the hind claw, not with his bill, as some people think. In most cases the game is struck senseless, and then the falcon drops down on it at once. Sometimes, however, when the falcon strikes her bird in the air, she flies off with it, and is then said to carry, which is rather a common trick of old birds. In some instances the bird, although struck, gets up again, and the hawk has to rise and swoop again; and in several instances during the day, as the partridge dodged about hedges, &c., a most exciting hunt took place—always, however, ending in the "who'-hoop." In case the falcon does miss his quarry, he is enticed back by the "lure," which is simply some partridge wings nailed on to a piece of wood, which, when thrown up in the air, causes the falcon to swoop down, when he is easily secured. Although a very wet day, which is always against the hawks, the whole of them behaved very well, rising splendidly. The hawk is always allowed to eat the partridge's head when a kill takes place. We have left out purposely a number of technical terms; but we hope the above short account will explain to the uninitiated the noble science of hawking as practised in these days.

CAPITAL RUN WITH C. MACDONALD MORETON
OF LARGIE'S OTTER-HOUNDS.

"'Tis pleasant in the woodland glade,
  Where the waving harebell grows,
Beneath the darkly chequered shade
  The startled game to rouse;
To wake the echoes far and wide,
  With hounds and bugle horn,
When on each tree and green hill-side
  Glitters the coming morn."

What can surpass the healthful enjoyment of field sports ?
Who is there acquainted with their many attractions, and
who can relish the excitement of those varied scenes of manly
diversion, who does not feel his heart bound within him at
their bare mention? Those who maintain that a moderate
share in their numerous attractions tends to debase the mind,
blunt the affections, and brutalize the disposition, must be
wholly unacquainted with the life of a true sportsman. A
taste for the pursuit of wild animals through magnificent
woods, over far-extended moors and mountains, on wide-spread
lakes, or on impetuous or peaceful rivers, is inherent in human
nature ; and this taste is never more strikingly displayed than
in the high spirits and joy evinced by the denizen of crowded
cities, whether he be a member of the "ring," a "bull" or a
"bear," a cotton broker, or any other man who has to keep
his nose to the grindstone, when they escape to spend, however brief, an interval amid those exhilarating scenes. The
"shop" is thrown aside (or ought to be), the cares and
anxieties of life are forgotten, their spirits become buoyant,
their strength is renewed, and they return to their several
occupations better and healthier men. Otter-hunting, above
all sports, is one to which the above remarks particularly
apply, as every one, without cost, from the peer to the peasant
can participate in the fun, if they have only a good pair of
legs, a stout heart, and strong lungs, so as to be able to stick
to the hounds, and see them working. The pursuit of the

otter, once a favourite sport, is now but little practised, on
account of the great scarcity of that species, almost all of
whom have been exterminated on account of their destructive
habits among the fish in our preserved waters. At this particular season of the year, when every other branch of the
chase is necessarily abandoned, it is not surprising that when
a pack of otter hounds appear in any district they are well
patronized. Otter-hunting, properly speaking, is now very
little understood, on account of the scarcity of packs, it being
a sport one reads about in books, but seldom sees. The otter
leaves a very strong and lasting scent, which seems to remain
much longer than that of either the stag, fox, or hare, and a
well-bred hound will challenge it twelve hours, if not more,
after the game has passed, which often accounts for the long
drags before a view takes place. On Saturday last I had an
opportunity of seeing a very good run with the above pack ;
and, although I am afraid my description of the sport will fall
very far short of those you have formerly had sent you from
the pen of an old and distinguished otter-hunter, still a short
account may interest some of your readers. The Meet was
Craigie old dam, at seven in the morning. A good field
turned out to meet the Laird, who is a thorough sportsman,
being master of fox-hounds in Ireland, as well as keeping this
pack. Amongst those present, I observed George Oswald,
Esq., of Auchincruive; Mr. and Mrs. Oswald, Yr., of Auchincruive, and Miss Oswald; R. H. Campbell, Esq., Yr., of Glendaruel; Colonel Campbell, C. Macpherson Campbell, Esq., of
Ballimore; Dr. Macknight, some officers of the 5th Fusiliers,
Messrs. White, J. Coats, Murray, Cross, &c., &c. Mr. Moreton
had six couple of otter hounds out, and two or three varmint
terriers. Punctually to the hour, Sandy cast the hounds on
the south bank, and, after feathering a bit, they crossed over
and opened underneath some trees.

> "Hark! on the drag I hear
> Their doubtful notes, preluding to a cry
> More nobly full, and swelled with every mouth ;
> As straggling armies at the trumpet voice,

Press to their standard, hither all repair,
And hurry through the woods, with hasty step
Rustling and full of hope; now driven on heaps
They push, they strive, while from his kennel sneaks
The conscious villain."

Somerville.

"Yoi him wind there, Chauntress! good bitch," cries the Laird, as they hunted it up the river. A little below Auchincruive the music increased, and away they went a burster, giving the field a sharp spin across the meadows. They then crossed the water—Colonel Campbell dashing in after them. It was a very pretty sight to see them carrying the scent over—speaking to it all the time. Going up the other side, the hounds feathered about a drain which the otter must have tried, but finding it shut, went on, as they picked up the scent over the river again, and some very pretty hunting took place through the beautiful policies of Auchincruive, the pace gradually increasing, it being a case of "bellows to mend" with some of the fat 'uns. "Hark! Sandy has viewed him," cries Moreton, and away we went helter-skelter down through a potato field, and, oh ye gods, what a crash there was. They had him in the water, but he slipped out. "Hoick, forward!" away again. "How well that young dog, Havelock, is working to-day," says Col. Campbell. "Have at him, Nigger, old boy," cries the Laird to his favourite hound. The whole pack were now rushing frantic for blood, but down the otter went again into a large and deep pool, near Gadgirth, only showing his snout above water now and then when he came up for air. "Try and stop him from going down the water," cries the Master, "and we must kill him," and in one moment down go Ballimore and Glendaruel into the pool to head him if he tries back. "Take care, Sandy," says the Colonel, as the huntsman in his excitement was very near going plump into a big pool, "we can't afford to lose a good man!" There was a little slow hunting here, as, from the size of the pool, it was difficult to force him to land. All of a sudden, a "View, hollo!" from the Laird announced that he had bolted from underneath some rocks

E

where he had lain down. The excitement was now intense, as they ran him almost in view down the banks of the river, but he slipped them again, and, crossing over, took up the opposite bank. After rattling him through the wood they fairly ran into him at the edge of the river—Mr. Moreton never resorting to the use of the spear. On looking at my watch I found we had just been three hours at it—no easy work, I can tell you. It would require the pen of a Campbell and the pencil of a Landseer to do justice to the scene, as Sandy stood in the wild glen with the otter over his head, the hounds all baying round, and the Laird giving his clear "Who'-hoop," the field all standing round in every variety of costume and colour, kilts, knickerbockers, trews, &c.; and I actually saw one gentleman with *lavender kid gloves on!* Mr. Oswald and young Mrs. Oswald having ridden down into the bed of the river, were just in the nick of time to see the death. "He must be twenty pounds weight," remarks Mr. Oswald, a good judge, having some years ago kept a pack himself. "Aye, and mair," says Sandy. As the morning was excessively hot, and the hounds had enough of it, the Master gave the word "Home," and away we trudged, somewhat leg-tired, excessively thirsty, and all highly delighted with the splendid sport we had seen. On the way home some of the Glaisca' drouthy ones, meeting a milk cart with rather a good-looking girl, took toll, and the amount of buttermilk imbibed was something fabulous, which, however, was pronounced perfect nectar, and sent them on their way rejoicing.

I hear this pack had another very good run on Monday, and a kill higher up the river; but as I had not the pleasure of seeing it, I am sorry I can't give you an account of the sport.

BRILLIANT TWENTY-FIVE MINUTES WITH THE LANARKSHIRE AND RENFREWSHIRE FOX-HOUNDS.

Tuesday, February 1.—Met at Bridge of Weir. Drew the strips above the village and Carruth blank; trotted back to M'Call's Covert, near Burnshields, where the "biggest fox that ever was seen" broke in view of the whole field, with the hounds at his brush. They went away at a perfect steeple-chase pace, and only those who had their eyes open when they found saw anything of this splendid burst. The fox went away north, past Lawmarnock, and on nearly to Barmuth Loch Dam, as if his point was Carruth. He then bent away west, pointing for Calder Glen, but changing his mind, "taking the privilege of the fair sex, although not a vixen," turned south. At this point a momentary check occurred, the hounds throwing up in a road; but hitting it off quickly again, they raced away past Barbeth and Auchincloich across the Locher Water; and then, leaving the Marshall Moor to the left, went over Barmaigh Hill to ground at Greenside—time, twenty-five minutes, with hardly what you would call a check, over a fine grass country, and the pace good enough for the greatest glutton; in fact, up to the check the hounds had rather the best of it. The first sixteen minutes, the cream of the thing, those who had the luck to get well away with the hounds and stuck to them, were Squires, Messrs. Orr, Thorburn, Couper, Hinshaw, Anderson, and two hard-riding young 'uns, Messrs. Collins and Dunlop, also a heavy weight on a bay, whose name I could not find out. Some other good men who ride to these hounds, although not in the first flight, were there or thereabouts.

LANARKSHIRE & RENFREWSHIRE FOX-HOUNDS.

These hounds began cub-hunting on the 11th September, and were out fifteen days in Lanarkshre, and twice in Renfrewshire, killing 11½ brace of cubs. They commenced the regular season at Houston Kennels on the 30th October, and have been out twelve times, killing eight brace, having been stopped by frost three days. Foxes were never more plentiful than they are this season in the best part of their country, Renfrewshire, and this may be attributed a good deal to the conciliatory manner Squires has with the keepers, as a word spoken in anger sometimes, although not intended, has been the death of many a fox. Squires has 31½ couple of working hounds, amongst which the following are as fine hounds as the keenest admirer of the noble science would like to see:— 7 years, Amazon, by their Rambler out of Actress, a fine old bitch; 6 years, Novelty, by their Marplot out of Nightshade; 5 years, Challenger, by Marplot out of Careful; Druid, by Fatal, out of Dainty; Garland, by the Brocklesby Gamester, out of Lord Fitzhardinge's Modish; 4 years, Wisdom, by the Belvoir Striver, out of Wishful; Monitor and Marmion, by Marplot, out of Matchless; Dexter and Tickler, by Fatal, out of Dainty; 3 years, Wanton and Wary, by Governor, out of Bridesmaid; Lowther, by Lictor, out of Artful; 2 years, Gratitude and Gossip, by Governor, out of Wisdom; Cardinal and Clasher, by Dexter, out of Careful; and 1 year—Bertram and Banker, by Dexter, out of Bravery. The same two whips that were with them last season continue on—namely, Harry Pacey and Geo. Bollen. The weather has been wretched since they began regular hunting, and Squires tells me that in all his experience, up to the present time, he never knew a worse scenting season. They have had nothing very much worth recording in the way of brilliant runs, but the following "spins" are worth laying before your readers:—

Nov. 27.—Met at Shelford Toll. Found plenty of foxes in Neilston Pad, but could not run them a yard, owing to a lifting frost. Trotted away to the gorse and the Craig of Carnock, where a brace, if not a leash, of foxes were at once on foot. One broke at the top side, and went away over a nice piece of country to Newton-Mearns, where they threw up. Squires, who was on foot drawing the rocks, met two couple of hounds coming back into the Craig with a fox, and thinking it was the hunted one, did not get away with the others; but when he got to his hounds, quickly cast them to the left, back over the road, where they picked it up, and hunted him down past Greenbank and Broom to the Rouken, where he went to ground. I noticed some of the officers of the 5th Fusiliers, at present quartered in Glasgow, out, who went well.

Saturday.—Met at Houston, always a favourite meet. Found a brace of foxes in the Scarth, and, after ringing round a bit, ran them into a drain. Found again at West Barlogan. He went out at the top end, as straight as an arrow, to Elphinstone, the hounds racing him, and only three or four who had their eyes open being with them—the gallant Master and Squires being "there." The fox never hung in covert, but went out at the top side over the country road and down to the left. Here they got on the line of a disturbed outlying fox, and ran heel down to his kennel, but Squires quickly lifted them, and cast over the road to the right, where they picked up the line of the hunted fox, and ran down to the Kilmalcolm Strips. He broke from here within a hundred yards of the hounds, and went away south, leaving Lawfield Gorse on the left, over the Knapps Muir back to West Barlogan, on to Emnely, going through the corner of the covert, went as straight as an arrow down to Bortherwickfield, which he did not enter, but went over the old steeple-chase course, all grass, up the hill through Clives (better known as Spiers' Young Covert). Then, leaving Drums to the right, went away for Barscube Hill, where they fairly ran out of scent. This was a very severe day, and although the latter part of the run was over a fine piece of country, horses and men were so beaten, having been at it for over two hours, that they were rolling about in all directions at the finish.

Saturday, 18 (Bishopton).—Found at once in the Ferry Wood. The fox broke away through Drums and right over Barscube Hill, where, a thick mist coming on, only those who were well with the hounds ever saw them again. The fox having lain down on the heather during the mist, was almost stept on by Mr. C. Couper's horse, when he jumped up, and went away down the hill a "clipper" to Finlayston, through which covert he went as far as the Broadfield boundary wall, and then, turning short back, they killed him at the low lodge— time 17½ minutes, without a check. Owing to the mist, only a few who were close to them when the fox jumped up on the moor saw anything of it, namely, Colonel Buchanan, Squires, Messrs. C. Couper, Campbell, Thorburn, Hinshaw, Holms, and Dr. Wolsey of the 5th Fusiliers.

LANARKSHIRE AND RENFREWSHIRE FOX-HOUNDS.

On Tuesday the 25th the above pack met at Crookston Castle, and had in the afternoon one of the best runs of the season. After drawing Crookston Wood blank—which was not to be wondered at, as they have killed two brace of foxes there this season—they trotted on to Hawkhead, a sure find, where a brace of foxes were at once on foot, one of which broke over the wall to the south, towards the Raise Wood, and then to ground. Went back to Hawkhead and got on the line of the other fox, but he was so dreadfully mobbed by the field that "Who'-hoop" was very soon the word. Here it would not be out of place to give a word of advice to a large number of persons who come out to hunt, subscribing nothing to the hounds, and deliberately riding over sown grass and wheat whenever they get a chance; in fact, going out of their way to do it, annoying the Master, and causing great damage. It would add greatly to their own safety, and the comfort of regular hunting men, if such parties would stick to the roads. After this little digression, we will proceed with our narrative. In going up to the first gorse at Fereneze, the farmer informed the huntsman that he had seen a fox come up from the Raise into the covert, and he proved to be correct, as the moment they were thrown in a fox broke towards Trees; the hounds flashed out to the north-east, but, swinging back, picked it up, and went away, leaving Trees to the left, down past West Arthurlie, round the bottom of the hill, passing Mains and Killoch; he then turned straight up the hill, as if his point was the Kippielaw, but did not go into the wood. Here some over-zealous riders went on along the road to the left, and, as the scent was rather catching, caused the hounds to swing too far to the south; but old Squires, by a judicious cast, hit it off to the west side of the Duchielaw, and away they raced, inclining rather towards Hawkhead. At a rather nasty boggy wall a member of the Hunt got a nasty fall, pitching on to his head in a bog, and came up, as poor Tom Oliver used to say, looking seven ways for Sunday. A slight check took place at a small water-course, but they got on his line to the left at once, and went away at a rattling pace for Gleniffer, near which wood the gallant Master got a nasty purl, his horse putting his foot in a rabbit hole, rolled clean over, but beyond a severe shaking, no harm was done. The fox here went down to the bottom of the covert, and broke at the Glasgow side, where a gentleman in a black coat, having had the luck to go down the hill, was seen sailing away with them all by himself. The hounds stuck to their fox here beautifully, hunting him in a most patient manner, through a severe storm of hail, down to Glenfield, and then straight up the hill to ground in a drain near Barrhead—time, forty-five minutes, with only one check to speak of. Up to Gleniffer—which was the cream of the thing—the most prominent men were Colonel Buchanan, Mr. Couper, on "Lottery;" Mr. Hinshaw, on "Budworth;" Mr. Addie, Mr. R. Kidston, Old Squires, and a very promising "young 'un," Mr. Dunlop, younger of Tollcross, who rides well and forward. As the day was very stormy, a number of sportsmen from Featherbedforshire had gone home before the run, which was much to be regretted, as they lost a very good thing.

CAPITAL DAY'S SPORT WITH THE AYRSHIRE HARRIERS.

Saturday, 28th March.—Met at the Wallace Monument, one of the highest points in Ayrshire, from which a magnificent view is to be had of the surrounding countries, with the bold peaks of Arran in the background. As it was generally supposed to be the last day of the season, a large field assembled to do honour to the popular Master, Mr. Ewen, amongst whom were the Marquis of Ailsa, the Earl of Eglinton, the Hon. Seton Montgomery and the Hon. Mr. Vernon, Capt. Tait of Millrig, Captain Neil and Lady, Captain Finnie of Newfield and Lady, the Misses Anderson, Mr. Adam, younger of Tour, and Miss Adam; Mr. Fairlie, younger of Coodham; Col. Hay Boyd, Mr. Cunninghame, Maulside; Mr. Kerr of Cunningham Hall; Messrs. Patrick, Boyd, Houldsworth, Chalmers, Kippen, &c. Before commencing the legitimate business, Captain Neil arranged to have a drag, which was well laid, under his direction, by Mr. Dunlop, over about five miles of a magnificent grass country, with only one ploughed field. They started in a large grass field at Midton, and went away a burster, leaving Fail Water to the left, where, in olden times, as Ramsay says in the "Evergreen,"

> "The Friars of Fail drank berry-brown ale,
> The best that ever was tasted;
> The Monks of Fail made very good kail
> On Fridays when they fasted."

From this the line lay past the rabbit wood on to Law, and up over Pisgah. Here, in a small spinney, a brace of foxes jumped up, and the hounds, changing from the drag, went away racing down the hill towards Little Foulton. Mr. Ewen, however, got them quickly stopped, and laid on the line again back at Pisgah, where they ran down the hill past Barnweill old church, and on to Craigie Byre to finish. As the day was intensely hot, a halt was now called, and an adjournment made to one of Captain Neil's farm-houses, where an excellent luncheon was provided for all comers. After the usual coffee-housing was over, a move was made to the meadows, where a hare was at once found at Midton. They went away at a great pace towards Caldrongill on to High Landside, from this to the left to Low Landside, and then down the hollow and up over Barnweill Hill. Here a slight check took place, as the hare turned sharp to the left down the road, and the hounds flashed over; but quickly getting on the right line again, they raced away up the hill to Craigie village, where she gave them the slip. The distance the hounds went was about four miles, with only one check, over the finest country in the world; and from the fact of Mr. Ewen's pack consisting chiefly of draft fox-hounds, the pace they went was tremendous, nothing but a well-bred one being able to live with them. Found another hare near Fail, and ran up to the monument, back down the hill, and killed— thus finishing as fine a day's sport as any one could wish for.

SPLENDID RUN WITH LORD EGLINTON'S FOX-HOUNDS.

With the exception of one or two small spins, these hounds have had little or no sport this season. On Tuesday, however, they had one of the best runs it has fallen to the lot of most sportsmen to see. The meet was Tawthorne Toll. After rattling them about a little in the morning, they found a real good "'un" in the Deane Covert. He broke over the road, pointing straight for Kilmaurs Mains. "Go along," cries Cox; "the beauties are streaming over the cream of the country, and catch 'em if you can." And sure enough it was a cracker, as they went almost straight as an arrow to Priestown (the best of them not being able to live with the hounds), where we believe he was brought to hand. Distance from find to finish, ten miles, with hardly what you would call a check. Although the hounds had rather the best of it, his Lordship

Cox, the Hon. G. Montgomerie, Mr. Richard Oswald, yr. of Auchincruive, Mr. J. Cunninghame, Mr. J. H. Houldsworth, and Mr. Middleton, of the 12th Lancers, were not very far off from the darlings. We hope that this run is only a beginning of many good things that we may have the pleasure of chronicling in the pages of the *Herald.*

LANARKSHIRE AND RENFREWSHIRE FOX-HOUNDS.

LAST DAY IN RENFREWSHIRE—RUN OF THE SEASON.

Tuesday, 10th.—Met at Crofthead, drew Glanderston Gorse, the Wauk Mill Glen, and Patterton round covert blank; but the moment the hounds were thrown into the Rouken, a sure find, a brace and a half of foxes were at once on foot, but, unfortunately, from the field surrounding the glen, a brace were chopped. While the funeral obsequies were being performed an old dog was viewed away over the Kilmarnock Road. Squires lost no time in getting on his line, and away they went a burster past the Cleugh and on to Greenbank, where the fox turned to the right, as if the Netherton Braes was his point, but, changing his mind, went straight up the country parallel with the Eaglesham Road, then, turning more to the right, he crossed the Earn Water near Hazletonhead, going round Hazleden, the residence of the indefatigable Secretary of the Hunt. Here he made a curious turn round Southfield House and back across the Clarkston Toll Road down to Mearns Castle, going back almost in a line with the road passing Kirkhill round Greenbank, and on leaving Capelrig to the left nearly to Patterton, where they fairly ran into him in the open. Time, one hour and ten minutes, with two small checks; distance, the way the hounds went, twelve miles. This was a very fine run, and if it had not been for a wire now and then, which gave the hounds rather the advantage, would have been perfect.

Tuesday, 17th.—Met at Gleniffer to finish the season in Renfrewshire. Found a brace of foxes in the Fereneze Gorse, and, after one or two very pretty rings round the hills, ran both to ground in some old drains. Went on to the Game Wood, and found at once. He broke at the south side, down the hill, past Low Capellie Farm-house. (Just as the hounds went away, an old and enthusiastic member of the Hunt got a bad fall, breaking his collar bone.) The fox then turned sharp up the hill, going straight as an arrow to Middleton Wood. Squires, getting first over a boggy ditch in the hollow, led with the hounds up to the top of the hill, where the most of the field got up, and met the hounds streaming out of the wood. He then raced away over the top of Corkindale Law, inclining rather to the left down to Loch Libo, where this gallant fox did not hang an instant, but went out at the bottom end to Caldwell, the hounds racing for blood. Being dead beat, he lay down in the new garden; but jumping up in view of the hounds, they raced him across the avenue, over the Lugton Inn Road and back again, nearly down to the inn, where they killed him. Time, thirty-eight minutes, without the semblance of a check, and all grass; distance, seven miles. This run was acknowledged by all those who had the good luck to be in it as the best of the season, being as straight as an arrow and all sound going, with no fences too big for either hounds or horses. A word of praise is due to M'Pherson, Mr. Graham's keeper, who admirably carries out his master's views with regard to always having foxes in his fine grass country.

THE SPORTING RUN WITH THE LOTHIANS FOX-HOUNDS.

Last week a large number of redcoats, accompanied by a sprinkling of the fair sex, assembled to meet the popular Master of the above pack at Bangour House. Amongst those present were two well-known members of a west country pack, who used to have very good sport with Jack Fleming and the Hon. Mr. Sandilands over this country in days gone by. I am informed that the field was in great luck, as the hounds had the best run that has taken place since Mr. Hope took the management of this pack. They found a " good 'un " at once in the old Bangour Covert. He went away due west, nearly to Cairnpapple, then turned up the hill to the right, where a slight check occurred. Up to this they had been going a cracker; time, sixteen minutes. They then went to the strips to the right of Wallhouse, and on to Lothcote, leaving Cochleroi to the right, and down towards Linlithgow; he then turned up again, going over a nice bit of country to Champ-fleurie, and bending away up hill they lost him. Time, from find to finish, one hour thirty minutes. It was stated by some of the old hunting men that the above run was one of the finest they have ever seen in this country.

LANARKSHIRE AND RENFREWSHIRE FOX-HOUNDS.

" Of all our British manly sports
Fox-hunting is the best;
In spite of wars and petty jars
That sport has stood the test."

I am sorry I have had so few opportunities of chronicling the doings over hill and dale of the above pack as yet; but the fact is the Fates have been against me. Never in the recollection of the oldest hunting man has there been such a season. Last year was bad enough in all conscience; but, with the exception of one or two good hunting days at the commencement of the season, the curlers have had it all their own way. Most unaccountably, at the beginning of the hunt-ing in Renfrewshire foxes were running about like rabbits, but latterly, although most of the keepers say they see a "tod" almost every day when they are out shooting, still, when the hounds come, they are *non est.* This may be accounted for by the fact that there are in Renfrewshire a great many capital outlying patches of gorse; and I think if Squires, instead of trusting too much to his regular coverts, were (as Lord Eglinton used to do) to draw his hounds oftener through such places, he might drop on a fox now and then.

Tuesday, 7th.—Met at Crookston, but the mist was so bad that, after waiting an hour, it. was no use, so home was the word.

Thursday, 9th.—A bye day at the same meet. Found in Crookston, and chopped. Went over to Hawkhead, where a fox was at once on foot. He broke across to Crookston, and on to Pollok, where he was lost. I am sorry to say that the whole of the fine Fereneze country was afterwards drawn blank.

Saturday, 11th (Bishopton).—This meet in olden times was generally considered the crack one of the season, but times have changed. Knockmountain is not as it used to be. Drew Erskine blank, but the keeper here had the misfortune to lose two foxes in the thaw, they having been drowned by the flooding of a drain. Trotted on to Westferry, which apparently was drawn blank, although it was reported a fox had been seen at the low end. A skedaddle took place from the covert after some young hounds "running riot," the field going off at a score, thinking it was a fox.

> "I can hardly describe all the frolic and fun
>   Which always takes place in the start for a run,
>   But must quote the old proverb, howe'er trite and lame,
>   That the foot-people often see half of the game."

When the hounds ran up into High Drums Covert a fox went away up through Park-Erskine Glen. Here a gentleman in black tally'd the fox, *in covert,* and turned him from his point, which was evidently Barscube. Going across Dargavel Burn he turned up to the right, leaving Corshe Covert, and went on to Elphinstone to ground. Very fast while it lasted.

I cannot understand why the earth here should not have been
stopped, as when the hounds meet at Bishopton, and draw
the coverts in the vicinity, a fox is generally forced to fly to
the high country. The rest of the day was spent in drawing
covert after covert blank. It was, however, a very raw, cold
day, with a good deal of snow in the high country, and " Mr.
Tod" may have been very sensibly underground.

A good deal of amusement was caused the Monday following by a man leading a fox by a string up and down past the
Western Club, a wag suggesting that no doubt he had heard
of the scarcity of that animal on the last day's hunting, and
had come to offer the fox to some prominent member of the
Hunt to ensure a find at their next meet.

Tuesday, 14th (Bridge of Weir).—The moment the hounds
were thrown into the long covert (East Torr) a brace, if not a
leash, of foxes were on foot, thanks to that keen preserver of
foxes, Mr. Graham—

> " Hark the loud peal begins the clamorous joy,
> The gallant chiding loads the trembling air."
>
> *Somerville.*

The fox went away east, leaving Bridge of Weir to the left,
and on over the Locher Water to what is known by hunting
men as M'Call's Covert; being headed here, he turned back
over a fine line of grass country with some thumping walls, and
was run to ground at Carruth. This was a very good twenty-
five minutes. Went back to East Torr, where a fox broke at
the east end, and went away over all those large grass fields on
to Auchincloich. Here he was coursed by a collie dog, turned
back to the hounds, and eventually run into the open, after a
good hunting run of forty minutes. Not content, Glentyan was
then drawn, from which they had a very smart spin of about
twenty minutes, and another kill in the open. Although this
was what may be called a " ringing day," still it was one of
the best they have had this season, as in all three runs they
had the hounds with them most of the time.

Thursday, 16th (Castlemilk).—Found in the banks as
usual. The general line of a fox from this covert is the

Castlemilk country, but on this occasion he went in quite a different direction, going away across the Cart, towards Busby. The first whip, Mr. J. Hamilton of Greenbank, and Mr. Collins got well over, but a well-known member of the " Glasgow iron ring," who followed, got into a hole (where I recollect seeing John Harrison nearly drowned long ago), and was left for drowned, the pace being too good to stop and pick him out; however, I am glad to say he got up to the hounds afterwards. The field all went round by the bridge at Lynn. The hounds went at a slashing pace over the road, leaving Williamwood to the right, on past Greenbank to ground at the Broom. George, the first whip, was the only man with them. It is a great pity the field did not "knick" in, as they went over a fine line, with, strange to say, little wire. Went back to Castlemilk, and had a very sharp burst up to Dechmont Hill, where they lost him. A new and keen member of the Hunt, mounted on the "Sard," went well in both runs; and I only hope that, although not a hunting man before, he having now tasted of the joys of the "noble science," will be keener than ever. Hoping that, now the mild weather has set in, I may have some good runs to chronicle in your pages, I can only wind up with the following lines:—

> "The dream is o'er; what more is in the chase,
>   'The love chase,' when all's o'er but a sweet dream!
> A dream in which the fancy *goes her pace;*
>   A dream of tree, and field, and sunlit stream,
> And gloomy hollows, where the fern decays,
>   Yet makes the foxes' solitude. I seem
> Lost in my vision. Off, light thoughts, begone!
>   'Tis but fox-hunting that I write upon."

LANARKSHIRE AND RENFREWSHIRE FOX-HOUNDS.

> "Though scarlet in colour our clothing,
>   Our pinks may be tinged in their hue,
> The red cap of liberty loathing,
>   Each sportsman's at heart a true blue;

Through life 'tis our sworn resolution
To stick to the pig-skin and throne;
We are all for a good constitution!
Each man taking care of his own."

The above lines, slightly altered from "Bailey," will, I think,
express the feelings of most sportsmen, and in spite of all the
Dilkes to the fore! there does not seem to be any falling off
in the followers of the most popular and health-giving sport
in the three kingdoms. Long may such be the state of
matters.

Tuesday, 1873.—Met at Castlemilk, where Captain Stuart
dispensed his usual hospitality; after which a move was
made to Netherton Braes, where they found at once, but,
unfortunately, the fox got to ground in the rocks. Drew
Castlemilk lower woods blank. A good number of foxes have
been killed hunting this year at Castlemilk, and even the
best coverts are sometimes blank from some unaccountable
cause. Every one knows, as I have had occasion to say
before, that Hunter is as keen a preserver as his master could
wish, so it is not his fault. Found in the "Muir" and ran
down to Cathkin, where he went to ground in a drain; after
an hour's digging he bolted, and Squires giving him good law,
they went away a burster up the hill, back to where they found
him. Disdaining, however, to enter the covert, and no doubt
being hard pressed, turned to the right, rather pointing
for Carmunnock, but went away towards Chapelhill and
crossed the Kittoch water; going along the banks he re-
crossed the burn, and turned up towards Limekilns, and
leaving the coverts on the right, crossed the Kilbride road,
and was run to ground in a drain quite close to Old Frams
house at Calderwood, just about ten yards in front of the
hounds. Time, forty minutes, without a check, over an entirely
grass country. But, alas! I have once more to condemn that
dreadful system of man-traps, namely, running wire through a
hedge which is hardly visible, until you are made aware of
the fact by a frightful "cropper." If it had not been for
these "stoppers," this run would have been perfect. Captain

Bunbury, Scots Greys, who went well, did a thing I have read about, but never heard authenticated. At one of the wire fences he got off, laid his red coat over the wire, and then led his horse over. Towards the finish the hounds rather split, but those who were first up when the fox went to ground were Messrs. Durham Kippen, Peter Whyte, John Reid, yr. of Gallowflat, A. Chalmers, Geo. Kidston, Captain Bunbury, and Mr. Stuart, yr. of Castlemilk. That veteran sportsman, Mr. A. Scott, also went well throughout. I was sorry to miss the face of a keen sportsman at the meet whom no weather ever stops. I hear he is temporarily confined to his room, but everyone hopes soon to see him again at the covert side.

LANARKSHIRE AND RENFREWSHIRE FOX-HOUNDS.

"I have lived my life, I am not yet done:
I have played the game all round;
But I freely admit that the best of my fun
I owe it to horse and hound."

Kilmalcolm, 30th November, 1873.—There was an old saying, "Out of the world into Kilmalcolm;" and for a great many years the village was one of the oldest-fashioned in Scotland. Since Col. Buchanan bought the Finlayston estate the aspect of affairs has completely changed. Most of the old hovels have been demolished, excellent houses erected in their place, and Kilmalcolm bids fair, from the salubrity of the atmosphere, and the easy access to Glasgow, Greenock, and Paisley, to become a rising locality. To show the antiquity of the old part of the village, I noticed one cottage with the date 1626 over the door. By the way, a good deal of mis-apprehension exists with regard to the meaning of the name Kilmalcolm, most people thinking that the name originally arose from the fact that St. Malcolm was a martyr in the locality. This, however, is a mistake. The name was originally "Kilmalcolm," or the burying-place of St. Malcolm.

G

But I am running away with the harrows. There was a very large field out, and I was very glad to see a number of young faces, who, I hope, although they may come to grief now and then at starting, will not give it up if they have one or two falls, but stick boldly to the noble science of fox-hunting. The Colonel intended to draw the Slates first, and then come round by Craigmarlock, but as the morning was so thick, Squires thought it would be better to take the other side of the country. Found at once in Auchenbothie Gorse; in fact, I viewed the fox away from the covert before the hounds were thrown in. He went back, however, and they ran him round the west end (where I think another fox went away to Craigmarlock), and he broke down the hill over a little boggy hollow as if for the strips, but went along the west side of the road, and up over the Kilmalcolm and Finlayston road, and tried the earth at Knockmountain. Finding no refuge there, he then went to the left, over the high part where the original covert was (rather a nasty drop to negotiate), and down over the above-mentioned hill to the west end of Finlayston, where they ran him to ground in the rocks above the Greenock road. This was a very pretty twenty minutes, and as hard as they could "leg" it all the way without a check. Trotted up to a small part of gorse, near what they call Brodie's Wood. It is a curious fact that, when the Colonel has been out shooting, he has invariably put out a fox from this whin; and just as Squires was going up to the covert, so sure was he that he would be at home, and afraid that he would chop him, cracking his whip, out he went like an arrow. The hounds ran him through Craigmarlock and down to the Dam. Leaving Castle Hill to the left, the fox went over the water. Here the field lost sight of the hounds, as they went round the side of a small hill on to Auchindores. The Colonel, thinking they were bending for Knockmountain, jumped into the road, and the field followed. At this point, the second whip, who had collected three couple and a half of hounds, must have headed him, and, riding down the Finlayston road, turned off to the right with these hounds. Seeing the whip, the Colonel thought he must have viewed the running hounds. This, however, was not the case. I viewed the body of the pack take their fox (which was only 150 yards ahead of them) up to Midhill Gorse. Galloping down the road, the field met the hounds coming down into West Finlayston, and here "Mr. Fox," as the writer of "Happy Thoughts" calls him, had a narrow squeak for it, as they were just at his brush. He managed, however, to give them the slip, and went away by Burnside over Barscube Hill, a regular pumper. Squires had a cropper here. His horse put his foot in a hole, stumbled, and the old gentleman rolled off, I am happy to say, without injury. While he was down, the Colonel offered to wait for him, but the old man, with his usual pluck, cried out, "Go on, Colonel; it will take you all your time to catch 'em." Going down the hollow there was some slow hunting, and a party from Paisley, on a "woe begone" jade, which looked as if he felt unhappy outside the knacker's yard, pressed the hounds. Squires cried out to him, "If you have a wife and family, for goodness' sake don't go so near my hounds, as, if you do, they will eat both your horse and yourself." But Mr. Graham's keeper hollo'd them on, and, going up through Muirtown, they ran him into Elphinstone. It is a question if they did not change foxes here. One broke as if for Clives, but, being headed, went back, and breaking at the same point, went up to the above-mentioned covert. Mr. Durham Kippen (who had a fall in the run, but, luckily, was not hurt) viewed him, and informs me that he thinks it was not the run fox that went on. The Colonel, however, tells me he is inclined to think that they must have changed in Elphinstone, as he viewed a fox dead beat before the hounds, and told the whip to be sure and stop them if they got on to the fresh fox. As bad luck would have it, however, the hounds slipped out at the east corner, and raced their fox back through Muirtown to ground at Clives. This was as fine an hour and a quarter as these hounds have had this year, and the scent was wonderful over every sort of ground. A word of praise is due to Mr. Hay, the Finlayston

keeper, for his excellent show of foxes, and he ably carries out
the views of the lessee of the shooting, to take care of them
like "babies." I am sorry to hear very bad accounts of
"vulpecidism" on the march of the county; but I am informed
that the statement made as to the number of foxes killed is
very much exaggerated. I have another grievance, "wire,"
which, I am sorry to say, is becoming prevalent in our best
country, and I can only conclude this account by Whyte
Melville's protest:—

> "You may bore the blackthorn and top the oak rail,
> Here courage can serve, and there craft can avail;
> The seasoned old horse does his timber with ease,
> The young 'uns jump water as wide as you please;
> But the wisdom of age, and the four-year-old's fire,
> Are helpless alike if you ride 'em at wire."

The above day's sport was, taking it all in all, one of the
best I ever saw; and my only regret was that the gentleman
with the umbrella arrived too late to see any of the fun.

BRILLIANT RUN WITH THE LANARKSHIRE AND RENFREWSHIRE FOX-HOUNDS.

SIR,—It is a curious fact that very often when the Colonel
takes the hounds down to Renfrewshire for a day's cub-
hunting they have a "clipper," and on Saturday last one of
the best runs took place over the cream of their country that
the Colonel tells me he has ever seen. The meet was
Kilmalcolm, and it was much to be regretted that there were
so few out even cub-hunting, as, although the ten o'clock train
to Kilmalcolm only stopped for riders, still, if they had con-
sulted their time tables, they would have found that Port-
Glasgow would have suited quite as well, as it is only about
three miles from there to Craigmarlock, the first covert drawn.
Did not draw Auchenbothie Gorse, but trotted on to Craigmarlock, where a brace, if not a leash, of foxes were on foot,

which were well rattled about, as also in the gorse above Finlayston, but without a "Who'-hoop." The moment the hounds were thrown into the east gorse above Finlayston House there was an immediate "chorus," and a fox broke straight up the hill to the west of Bogside Farm, and going to the east of Knockmountain, he turned up over Barscube Hill to the north of the Eden Farm. Then going along the north side, the Colonel thought he went into the top side of Park Erskine Glen, above Drums; and not wishing to disturb Mr. Graham's coverts, he and the field following rode down the glen on purpose to stop the hounds; but the hunted fox had never gone into the covert, but just skirting the top end turned sharp to the right, and nine and a-half couple of hounds raced him through Muirtown Covert on to Elphinstone. Here Squires lost his running hounds. Standing on the highest point of Knockmountain, Mr. Aitken's keeper (a keen preserver of foxes) and myself, on foot, were astonished to see the nine and a-half couple come racing down the hill from Elphinstone without a soul near them. Crossing the Dargavel Burn, they then ran up along the wall that leads up to the road, down to Finlayston, as if the fox was going back to his old quarters; but turning to the left, they crossed the hollow, and casting our eyes forward, we viewed a small dark coloured fox making for the gorse; but seeing us as he turned round the bottom, not going up to the main earth, he went on down through the hollow up to the strips, and, leaving the Doctor's house to the right, went away to the left of the village of Kilmalcolm, and was run into just a little above the Buchanan Arms, without a rider within five miles of them. Young Mr. Stoddart (Broadfield), happening to be coming up from the train, saw the "kill," and picking up the fox, went away in search of Squires; but I have not heard as yet if he fell in with him. The event caused quite a sensation in the village. Up to Park Erskine Glen there was no check and all grass, and the Colonel and Mr. D. Kippen, who were in it, inform me that it was as nice a twenty-five minutes as they have ever seen in

Renfrewshire, and all the hounds up, which is saying a great deal for young 'uns. I can say that from the time I saw them coming over the hill from Elphinstone they never had a semblance of a check, and the time from find to finish would be about fifty minutes. From what I hear, some of them had quite enough at Drums from the pace they went, and I doubt very much if any horse could have lived with them to the finish. Colonel Buchanan was within a hundred yards of his "beauties" all the way to where they were thrown out; and Mr. George Kidston, Mr. Durham Kippen, and young Mr. Arthur were in their usual places. The opening meet of the above pack will take place here, to-day, at the Kennels, an account of which I hope to give in your next edition.

SPLENDID RUN WITH THE LANARKSHIRE AND RENFREWSHIRE FOX-HOUNDS.

Saturday, 8th March.—Met at Bridge of Weir; one of the largest fields I have seen this season, the Meet being graced by an unusual number of the fair sex. The morning was everything that a sportsman could wish for, and the universal remark was, "There must be scent to-day." As old John Harrison used to say, "Scent, sir, is a thing nobody knows anything about till they try;" and my advice to young sportsmen is always to say, "I think the scent will be bad to-day," and if their predictions don't turn out correct so much the better. Old John was right when he stated scent was an enigma. I have seen hounds at Shotts running with a breast-high scent over "*snow*" in the open, and when they went into covert, where the snow was melted, throw their noses up. Again, I have seen them running in the open, where the snow was lying, hardly speaking to it, and whenever they went into covert where snow was lying, racing after their fox; such is scent, and on Saturday we had a very good idea of this. Drew the Scarth and West Barlogan blank, but a fox jumped up on the Knapps Muir, and ran to ground in the

hollow, supposed to be a vixen. Found again in Lawfield
Gorse, and ran with a catching scent round by Ennely towards
the Scarth, and on to Botherwick Field, where they lost him.
Drew the Wreas, Muirtown, and Elphinstone blank, but there
seemed to be a slight "drag," as the hounds feathered every
now and then, as if a fox had gone away before them; however, they made nothing of it. Went back to Corslie Gorse,
on the Barrochan estate, where, it is needless to say, Scott has
always a fox, and of course he was at home. The fox broke
at the top end, and went up towards Muirtown; leaving this
covert on the left, he then bent away down over the Dargavel
Burn, and up over Barscube Hill. Some of those who had
been racing "jealous" pretty well pumped. In going down
on the other side, Mr. Wallace, the sporting Glasgow dentist,
who seems to lead a charmed life with hounds (although, I
must say, always riding good cattle), jumped a wall with a
wire along the top, stumped the field, and had it all to himself
down to Westferry. After crossing Barscube, the line lay past
Gleddock. Not hanging in the Ferry Wood, this gallant fox
went straight on to Castle Hill, and leaving Drums to the
right, went down the hollow over a magnificent bit of country,
and was run to ground in a drain at Dargavel; time, fifty
minutes, without a check. Those who were in the cream of
it were—Col. Buchanan, up to Barscube, Messrs. D. Kippen,
Watson, P. White, Wilson, Hunter, Smith, W. S. Stuart, yr.
of Castlemilk, J. Hill, George Kidston, A. Crum, and a well-
known old sportsman. A ludicrous incident happened to Mr.
Watson's hunter on the way back. The horse, being taken
suddenly with an attack of the megrims, lay down, and made
vigorous efforts to depart this life; so much so, that Mr. Watson
walked home, and sent his servant down to report progress.
The servant returned and said the horse was "defunct," and
the only thing that was wanted was a knacker cart!
However, during dinner a messenger came up, and reported
the horse had *come to life again;* and after being judiciously
treated by young Mr. Cockburn, V.S., is now, I am happy to
say, all right.

LANARKSHIRE AND RENFREWSHIRE FOX-HOUNDS.

"There are soul-stirring chords in the fiddle and flute,
  When dancing begins in the hall,
And a goddess in muslin, that's likely to suit,
  Is the mate of your choice for the ball;
But the player may strain every finger in vain,
  And the fiddler may rosin his bow,
Nor flourish, nor string, such rapture will bring
  As the music of sweet Tally-ho!"

I can imagine some of your fair readers perusing the above verse of Whyte Melville's, and saying, "There's that rude Stringhalt putting fox-hunting before dancing;" but I can assure the dear creatures that this is far from my intention. I have always found that genuine sportsmen, and especially fox-hunters, are most assiduous in their attention to the fair sex; and whenever their services are required in getting up assemblies, &c., &c., it is never "hoick-back," and most of 'em can hold their own when "tripping the light fantastic toe" against the majority of the "Jeunesse dorè" who do not hunt. I must now struggle through an account of the "run of the season," and it is with a good deal of difficulty I do so, as, having had the pleasure of writing so many accounts of sport with these hounds this season, it is difficult to vary one's accounts.

Saturday, 11.—Met at Craigends—one of the largest meets I have seen this season. After partaking freely of the hospitality of the Laird, Squires trotted off, and drew the west covert blank. Just as he had drawn his hounds out, and was going towards the north covert, he cried to the Colonel, "I think I heard a hollo! sir." It appears that the footpeople had disturbed the covert, and a fox had broken away down the avenue and through the lodge gate. Although hardly applying to this run, I cannot help quoting again from Melville—

" A fox for a hundred! they know it the pack,
    Old "Chorister" always speaks true;
And the whip from the corner is told to come back,
    And forbid to go on for a view.
Now, the varmint is spied as he crosses the ride—
    A tough old campaigner I trow—
Long, limber, and grey, see him stealing away,
    Half a minute! and then Tally-ho!"

The moment the hounds went out at the gate they picked it up, ran up the road a little, and then turned to the right, round the back of Houston House; and going through the small plantation, they crossed over the bye-road from Houston to Barrochan, and raced over to the main road, leaving the farm-house to the left, where at our first steeple-chases we used to get weighed. The fox then bent up towards Clives, but turned down to the left, and went over the old steeple-chase ground across the Wreas Road, down over a rather nasty bit in the hollow to Botherwickfield. Up to this point they had been going a " clipper;" but as the fences were small, most of the field managed to live with them. The fox did not hang in covert, but broke away to the right, and, leaving Ennely to the left, went up the hill to the Wreas. "Hoick-forrard," no chance of getting a pull at your horse, as they went on without a check down through the stacks at Shovelbread Farm to Muirtown. The hounds went through the north end and up to Elphinstone. A number of the field at this point, not being very well forward, rode straight through Kilallan old wood up to Elphinstone, and "knicked" in. The hunted fox did not go into the covert, but turned to the right (a fresh fox jumped up on the moor above Elphinstone, " Chorister" and another hound going away with him to the Kilmalcolm strips), went down over the Dargavel Burn, up over Barscube Hill, and down through Netherton Covert to West Ferry, where this gallant fox saved his brush by going to ground; being completely out of the country which the Colonel intended drawing, the earths were open. It was generally agreed that this was *the* run of the season. Time, fifty minutes; distance eight miles, with hardly what you would call a check. The hounds flashed out at Botherwickfield, and there was a slight check above Elphinstone; but if it had not been for these "pauses," nobody would have been able to keep up with the hounds, owing to the state of the country. Up to the Wreas there is no doubt the Colonel could not be caught, "besting" most of the "fast 'uns." The Lord-Lieutenant was in his usual place at the finish; and his eldest son, Hugh, went like a sportsman from find to finish, and was never very very far off the "darlints." Long may we have the same class of young men to ride straight, and lend us a hand in promoting the noble science of fox-hunting. Amongst the new division, young Mr. Muir and Mr. M'Farlane went well. The old hunting division, whose names it is unnecessary to mention, were in their usual position. I would offer a word of advice to some of the new men out this year. Some of the old members have informed me that several of them (of course through ignorance) are in the habit of "rushing" at gaps, getting over first, and then spurting up the next field, I have no doubt thinking they were doing a great thing. I would advise such gentlemen to be a little modester until they learn a little more about hunting.

Some of the Ayrshire division were out, and were highly pleased with the run; and Major Naper of the 11th, well known as a first-class man with hounds in all countries, and taking a line of his own, was well in at the finish, told the Colonel it was as good as he had seen. Just as the hounds went away, Mr. George Dunlop, Tollcross, got a bad kick, and suffered a good deal; but although having to get off, with his indomitable pluck he was hoisted into the saddle and rode on. Although suffering a good deal of pain, I hear to-day there are no bones broken, andt bat he is going on well; and all members of the Hunt will be glad to see such a good 'un again in the saddle, going in his usual form.

LANARKSHIRE AND RENFREWSHIRE FOX-HOUNDS.

"Rouse, boys! rouse, 'tis a fine hunting morning;
Rouse! prythee, rouse, let us on to the chase;
Let not the time fly whilst you're adorning,
But onwards to covert fly at a brisk pace."

I did not expect to have the pleasure so soon of again giving an account of the doings of this pack; but it never rains but it pours, and really runs are now coming fast and furious, to make up for lost time.

Saturday, 18th (Howwood Toll).—Found at once in the Skiff Wood. After ringing once or twice round the covert, the fox broke at the east end above the rocks pointing to Loch Libo, but bent away rather to the right round to South Castle Walls, and straight on to Overtoun, as if his point was now Caldwell. Being headed here, he turned sharp back by Springside, and down over the road to the Bleachfield. Going round Easterhill, he then went to the left towards the Brimmer, and was run into in the open above Belltrees. Time, thirty-five minutes, without a check. This was a very fine run for hounds, but some nasty boggy places at starting prevented most of the field from getting well away with them. Just as the hounds went away, whilst the riders were going through a gate at a farm-yard, a person rushed out and tried to stop them, and even went the length of catching the reins of an old and respected member of the Hunt; however, a "doughty champion," from the "middle of Renfrewshire," jumped off his horse, and the obnoxious individual was soon disposed of, the riders getting through. As the only field they went over was unsown plough, there could not possibly have been any damage done.

Found again in Bardrain young covert, and had a very sharp burst on towards the Skiff, down through Johnstone young covert, and back up the hill again, where, as it was getting late, they whipped off.

Tuesday, 21st (Darnley Toll).—Found in the Waulkmill Glen, and went away at once up the hill to Lyoncross Farm. Then, going over the road, they went round the Balgray Reservoir, on past Netherton and Balgraystone to the Craig of Carnock, the fox evidently intending to try the earths. Up to this point it was as straight as an arrow, and only those who were on the south side of the glen got well away with them, namely, the Colonel, Messrs. D. Kippen, Monteith, Davies, 5th Fusiliers; Jackson, and young Cockburn the vet. A slight check took place at the road close to the rocks, which let the field up. The Colonel, by a clever and quick cast, swung the hounds round back over the road, and away they streamed again across the hollow.

> " The jack-snipe started from its dream,
> The pee-wit answered with a scream;
> Round and around the sound was cast,
> Till echo seemed an answering blast."

The line now lay over the Walton Burn, and down over a nasty wire fence into the road. Going on past Craigton, the fox went over the Middleton Muir to the Dod Hill, where they killed him. This was a very fast thirty minutes, with only one check, and by some was considered very nearly as good as the opening day.

Saturday, 25th (Broadfield).—Drew the Devol's Glen blank, but found in the gorse above Finlayston. Ran down into the low wood and lost. A well-known member of the Hunt, who generally goes very straight, was accused of heading the fox, but from my "Mount Pisgah" view I thought others were to blame as well as him. Drew Knockmountain and adjacent gorses blank; however, at this season of the year it is uncertain where to find foxes, as they are generally going in pairs, and, sure enough, whenever the hounds were thrown into the Kilmalcolm strips, three foxes were viewed away by some labourers draining. The hounds settled down to one, and raced across the hollow, up to Knockmountain. As they went into the gorse they divided, four couple of hounds turning down the hill, but the body of the pack and the field

went right over the old covert and down across the road
nearly to Castlehill Farm, where a check took place. Squires
cast them forward, when they picked it up again and ran
down into Finlayston and lost. It is a singular thing how
often a fox is lost here; but there may be "reasons," as there
are capital breeding earths here, and it is getting late in the
season.

Tuesday, 28th (Hawkhead).—A lawn meet, where Lord
Glasgow, with his usual kindness, although not himself present, provided a most *recherché* hunt breakfast for all comers,
and an invitation, if anywhere near about luncheon time, to
pop in again. Found a brace of foxes in Crookston Wood,
one of which, after running up to the top of the covert, was
headed by the gentleman on the ride, turned back, and broke
at the bottom end. Leaving the burn to the right, he went
on to the Barrhead Road; but being headed here, turned to
the right into Hawkhead, round the back of the stables, and
over the Park wall. Unfortunately, the small wooden gate
between the two policy gates was locked, and Squires had to
take his hounds round, which must have given the fox at least
ten minutes' start. However, Squires, by a judicious cast got
on his line again, and they went away, leaving Logansraes to
the left, over the Paisley Road, very nearly to Glenfield, as if his
point was Gleniffer. Changing his mind, however, he then went
straight up the hill, over a fine grass country, to the Duchielaw
new covert, and then on to Capellie Plantation, generally called
the Game Wood. Here he must have waited for the hounds,
being rather beat, as when he broke on the south side they
went away a burster, and, turning down the road to the railway, went up the hill, and was killed in the open, near
Shelford Toll. Time, one hour twenty-five minutes. Although
not a racing pace, this was a very fine hunting run, and very
nearly straight. With the exception of one young hound,
every hound was up at the death.

The brush was presented to Mr. John Hamilton, of Greenbank, an old member of the Hunt, who used to keep a capital
pack of harriers in the Mearns country.

Those gentlemen who knew old Kemp, and recollect the wonderful performances, for a man of his age, after the hounds on foot, would be repaid by a visit to the shop of Mr. Dougall, gunsmith, 23 Gordon Street, where there is at present a life-like bust of the old man, done by a local artist, Mr William Houston, 328 St. Vincent Street. Subscriptions for the bust will be received at the shop.

EXTRAORDINARY LONG HUNTING RUN WITH THE LANARKSHIRE AND RENFREWSHIRE HOUNDS.

March 22nd, 1873.—I have had the pleasure of writing so many accounts of "good things" with the above pack this season that I am afraid your readers must be beginning to tire of reading them; but I think the sport of Saturday last is almost unprecedented in the annals of the Lanarkshire and Renfrewshire Fox-hounds. Saturday, 18th, met at Finlayston, one of the estates of the esteemed Master of the Hounds. The mansion-house and shootings on this estate, most sportsmen will be glad to hear, have been leased by that genuine sportsman, Mr. George Kidston. It is needless to say that Hay has always plenty of foxes, and the moment the hounds were thrown in the east gorse a leash were on foot. One broke to the south and went up over the hill, another went on towards Westferry, with two or three couple of hounds. In the meantime the body of the pack were running a fox towards the house. This fox crossed out over the road near the smithy and went up the hill, leaving Knockmountain on the right. The fox then went away with turned back to Finlayston, and the hounds flashing a little crossed the line of the one which went away from the east end, and ran him over Barscube Hill on to Elphinstone to ground. Trotted back to Finlayston, and chopped a fox in the West Covert. Found again in a small gorse near the railway above Broadfield, and came away at a rattling pace through the north corner of Craigmarlock, down over the Greenock Road, up by Auchenbothy Gorse, and ran into him near Knockmountain. This was a very sharp fifteen minutes. Just as they were running into their fox, Mr. D. Kippen flew a high wall up hill with a paling on it, all the rest of the field going through a gate. As they were on their way home, most of the field having had plenty, a young sportsman, who never cries "enough," requested Squires to make one more draw, and he ran his beauties through Park Erskine Glen, Drums, at 4.10, when the "biggest fox that ever was seen" jumped out of the top strip. Crossing back down over the glen, he went up over the left shoulder of Barscube Hill, and going down over the Dargavel Burn went round the Wreas side of Muirtown, on to Elphinstone. The fox then turned to the right, ran down to the Kilmalcolm strips, and up over Knockmountain. Going straight again back over Barscube, he went up the hill the second time to Elphinstone. Never hanging in covert, although the earth was open, this gallant fox went on, leaving Lawfield Gorse to the right, over High Barlogan, down through West Barlogan; doubling back he came out at the east side, and going through Ennely, went on to the Wreas, where, as it was getting late, and both hounds and horses were completely "baked," Squires stopped the hounds; time, one hour and twenty-five minutes; distance, about twelve miles. Although it was a sort of ring, still they hardly ever checked, but hunted steadily in covert and out of covert all the time, showing that the Colonel's hounds can both race and hunt. The only four that saw the finish were Mr. George Kidston, Mr. W. Campbell, younger of Tillichewan, Mr. J. Wallace, and Squires (who got to his hounds at High Barlogan). Mr. George Smith, Mr. Muir, Mr. Stewart, Mr. William Finlayson, and young Mr. Arthur, went well as long as they could.

The Clydesdale Beagles, I am informed, had a very good run on Saturday, and accounts from other packs state that there was a wonderful scent in the afternoon.

LANARKSHIRE AND RENFREWSHIRE FOX-HOUNDS.

"Listening how the hounds and horn
   Cheer'ly rouse the slumbering morn,
From the side of some hoar hill
   Through the high wood **echoing shrill.**"

Milton.

"All hail" the commencement once more of the noble sport of fox-hunting; and although we have only been at the cubs as yet, still, is there any true sportsman's heart that does not rejoice at once more being able to participate in the "sport of kings, the image of war, and only five-and-twenty per cent. of the danger." It is not everybody, if they wish to do so, can play at billiards, cricket, or croquet; but there are very few, from the prince to the peasant, that cannot enjoy a bit of hunting. The cripple on his crutch, the sweep on his "moke," the elderly gentleman on his cob, the pedestrian, the fair sex, and the scarlet-coated subscriber, can all enjoy the exquisite joys of the hunting field; and although those may be found who, from ignorance, denounce fox-hunting, the chase will always find favour as long as horse and hound are available for the recreation of man—

"Till a' the seas gang dry, **my dear,**
   And the rocks melt wi' the sun,
I will loo' thee still, my dear,
   While the sands o' life may run."

What grander sight for any one's eye than a meet of fox-hounds—and may we never lose it! Where can coolness and courage be exhibited to greater perfection than the sight of a first-flight man taking a line of his own over a stiff country?—and where will you see such nerve and pluck? How can he tell what is on the other side of every fence?—but he resolutely throws his heart over and jumps after it. In the words of an old sportsman:—

"Oh! if there be in this earthly sphere
   A moment of bliss a sportsman holds dear,

> 'Tis the last big fence in a run without pause,
> That makes a man chance his neck in the cause."

Col. Buchanan has as yet confined his operations mostly to his own district, where there has been a very fair show of cubs; and a word of praise is due to Capt. Colt, Gartsherrie Cottage, and Mr. Jackson, Calder Park, for their excellent show of foxes. Old Squires comes out again like an evergreen, as he is, and it would have done anybody's heart good to have seen him the other day, like a two-year-old, on the steep bank at Calder Park, amongst the "darlints," working his fox. I am glad to see that old sportsman, John Hendrie, out again; and his "fidus Achates," James Paul, the best of servants, is all there. I am sorry to report no great addition to the rank on the part of the "Jeunesse doré" of Glasgow, two to one bar one, and the "field a pony," seems to please them better. Lord Eglinton opens on Friday the first November, and the Colonel on the Saturday following, when I hope to be able to give your readers further particulars as to the results of the cub-hunting season.

> "They may rail at this life—from the hour I began it
> I have found it a life full of kindness and bliss;
> And until they can show me a happier planet,
> More social and bright, I'll content me with this.
>
> "As long as one has a strong back and good thighs,
> And can follow the chase, altho' on their feet,
> They may say what they like of the sport in the skies,
> But *terra firma's* the place with a pack that is fleet."

SPLENDID SPORT WITH THE LANARKSHIRE AND RENFREWSHIRE FOX-HOUNDS.

> " The steady bay bearing the huntsman well—
> Within the covert Squires' inspiring cheer,
> The nervous sterns shaking the dull green dell—
> The anxious skirter of the copse appears!

I

> But hark! the deep unerring tongue, the bell
>   Of the dark wood, proclaiming sport is near!
> And the view hollo! when the skulker makes
> Down the dry ditch, and pressed the open takes."
>
> *Bulteel.*

Tuesday.—Met at Crookston. Sharp frost, and not a very large field, so many horses having been "baked" in the long run on Saturday. *Apropos* of this, there is a well-known sporting dentist in Paisley, who goes as long as he can; although his weight prevents him being a first flight man, the spirit is willing, and he generally manages to see a good deal, from his knowledge of the country:—

> " Some good fellows there are, unpretending and slow,
>   Who can ne'er be thrown out, cos they ne'er mean to go,
> And oftentimes, when the run's over, these tell
> The story much better than those who went well,
> For we're all of us thrown out in turn."
>
> *Warburton.*

The same gentleman having nicked in near the finish on Saturday, found a young gentleman lying down beside his horse (a young 'un), did the good Samaritan in the shape of a few *hatfuls* of cold water, and I am informed that both horse and rider are still in the land of the living. However, "hark back" to our run. The morning was very misty, and there was a doubt if it "*would do.*" A good deal of chaff took place while Squires was waiting till the mist cleared off. The promising young 'un, riding up to an old member of the Hunt who was riding a very mealy-faced grey roan, asked him the price of soap, as it appeared his horse's face had not been washed lately. A young member asking Squires why he did not begin, he said, "Well, sir, if you will kindly hang a lantern on to the tail of Mr. Kippen's horse, perhaps I might." (The bay in question had his tail up, and belonged to one of the straightest riders and genuine sportsmen in the hunt.) But *revenons a nos mouton.* The moment the hounds were thrown into Crookston Wood a fox was on foot, and after a ring or two I viewed him away. He was a "big 'un" in this instance, there was no mistake; but in most

instances, when anybody sees a fox, he generally is described
as the biggest fox ever was seen. Ran him over to Hawkhead, and lost him. Drew the Wreas blank. Roedeer
running about like rabbits, and during a little bit of riot, a
neighbouring farmer informs me he viewed two foxes go away
to the high country. Squires took his hounds away up the
hill to the Duchielaw Gorse, and found at once. Away he
went a cracker, making a ring round to Gleniffer. Skirting
the covert, the fox then went along the face of the hill, over
some beautiful grass country, and down a steep part, where
it was anything but child's work, down to Newton Wood—
generally known by old hunting men as Spiers' Covert—
lying just above the village of Elderslie, on the Johnstone
Road. Here they must have changed foxes, the run fox
having been seen going out at the west end towards Milliken.
The hounds, however, went away up the hill to the left, past
Bardrain, and away over a fine grass country, as if he was
making for Loch Libo; but as it was getting dark, with a
fresh fox, Squires gave it up, both hounds and horsemen
having had enough. The time from find to finish would be
about an hour, and they were going all the time.

LANARKSHIRE AND RENFREWSHIRE HOUNDS.

Saturday, January 5, met at Bishopton. After those who
had been at the Gaelic Club ball the night before had re-
freshed themselves at "our obliging hostess of the Bishopton
Inn," where the B. and S. was served by her bonnie daughter,
a move was made for West Ferry. The moment the hounds
were thrown in a fox broke at the west end, and went away
with the hounds at his brush (most of the field being left
behind), as if pointing for Finlayston, but, being hard pressed,
he turned to the left towards Knockmountain. The hounds
here flashed over the bye-road down to Finlayston, near the
small cottage where the "yelping collie lives." But Squires

quickly cast them back, and they raced up the road to the right, down over the Dargavel Burn, and across the boggy hollow, where most of the "funkers" were left behind. The line then lay up the hill, and leaving Muirtown to the left, they raced away over the hill to the west side of Elphinstone, which covert he disdained to enter, but going straight on, they lost him at Lawfield Farm-house. Squires cast the hounds on over the road towards the gorse, but could make nothing of it. In coming back, the hounds feathered all round the farm-house, as if the fox, who must have been dead beat, had taken refuge there. A "buxom" lassie appearing at the door, one well-known member of the Hunt asked her if she had seen the "tod." She at once answered, "Would ye like to ken?" and I have my suspicions that the said bonnie lassie had taken compassion on poor foxy, when he ran into the barn, and had locked the door! I have no doubt she would let him out to fight his battles o'er again. Colonel Buchanan, Mr. C. T. Couper, Mr. Wallace, and Squires, were the only four that got away well and lived with them to the finish. Mr. G. Dunlop, Tollcross, and Mr. James Couper, had about the next best position; but great were the disciples of "Macadam," taking a survey of the country about two miles off the hounds. The distance from point to point would be, without exaggeration, five miles, and quite straight, with only one "flash;" the only regret being that a number of good men and straight riders did not get away with them, and as the pace was so terrific there, had no chance of catching them up.

LANARKSHIRE AND RENFREWSHIRE FOX-HOUNDS.

"But can the eye pause on the pictured sheet?
The Colonel's hounds—the strong, the staunch, the fleet—
Come trotting to the Meet, amidst the February haze,
And coats get reddening with light—'The Meet'
At the brown covert side—the day of days
Rises and lives in all its life before us,
And hope, with breath suspended, waits the chorus."

Saturday, March 4.—Met at Linwood. Drew the Moss blank, but this was not to be surprised at, as the keeper at Burnbrae got no notice to stop his earths. Found at once in Craigends. The fox broke as if for Linwood, but turned to the left over the Gryffe, went up the Barrochan Burn, on through the north covert to the small toll near Drums, but turned back, and was killed on the road near the north covert at Barrochan. A brace of foxes went away to the high country with two or three couple of hounds, showing there is no scarcity of the "wily" in Scott's district. Trotted back to Houston Wood, where a fox was at once on foot. After ringing round the stables, he broke over the old steeple-chase ground.

> "The hounds are well laid on, save two or so,
> And these are soon whipped to their music too;
> The riders dash, the Colonel these retard,
> In mild requests that —— will hold hard."

The Colonel thought at first that the hounds had flashed outside the covert, and sent Mr. Collins and Mr. Arthur to turn them, but Miss Hinshaw, who happened to be driving past at the time, viewed a fox over the road, and told them the hounds were right. These gentlemen did not stop, but went on with the leading hounds round by Clives down to Barrochan, the field being a mile behind them. Two foxes came into the covert at Barrochan, the hounds going on with one to Park Erskine Glen, and down to West Ferry. Here the earths were open, why, I cannot say, and some foxes on foot went to ground. The run fox being out of his latitude, and not knowing the earths, went on. Going out at the west end of the Ferry Wood, he turned up by Barscube Hill, and then, bending away round by Barrochan, was killed in Houston Wood.

> "The coats, dyke-stained, here almost ceased to blush,
> But all are revelling over speed and death!
> No one in modern days regards the brush,
> So that Fox-Coke, the great Lord Nimrod, saith,
> I do not this as an improvement hail,
> For, like O'Connell, I would have my 'tail.'"

This was a very fine hunting run, and quite fast enough during part of it for the best of them. Down to West Ferry it was pretty straight, and the Colonel, Squires, Messrs. R. Kidston, Smith, Thorburn, Hunter, and Donaldson were well up.

Tuesday, March 7th.—Met at Castlesemple. Found in M'Call's Covert, and went away a regular burster through the Torr, on to Carruth. Going through this covert, the fox went up in the direction of the moor, and then turned to the right down to Duchal. He then came along the face of the hill, and was run to ground near the Bridge of Weir. The first part of this run was a steeple-chase, as the hounds had a breast-high scent over a grass country, with severe fencing. Mr. Couper and Messrs. Coats and Thorburn were not far off the darlings during the best part of it. Of course, the Colonel and Squires were in their usual places.

LAST DAY OF THE SEASON WITH THE LANARK-SHIRE AND RENFREWSHIRE FOX-HOUNDS.

Saturday, April 8.—Met at Bridge of Weir. A regular summer day, more like yachting than fox-hunting. Drew the Torr, Carruth, and Barr Craig (M'Call's Covert) blank, then went over to the other side of the country, where they drew the Scarth blank also; but in crossing the low end of the Knapps Muir a fox jumped up in view of the hounds, and went away a buster through West Barlogan and out at the east side. Going past Ennely Farm-house, he went on to Botherwickfield. Here a slight check took place, but they picked it up again at once, and raced away over the old steeple-chase ground, splendid going, past Gryffe Rays, on over the Bridge of Weir road, leaving Goudylee to the left, to ground at the Mines. Time, twenty minutes; distance, about four miles. This was one of the prettiest spins they have had this season, as the fox crossed the cream of the country. Up to the check, Mr. C. T. Couper, Mr. George Dunlop, and Mr. T. Thorburn had much the best of it. The hounds have been out sixteen days cub-hunting—killed fifteen brace and ran two and a half brace to ground; fifty days' regular hunting —killed sixteen and a half brace and ran nine brace to the ground. Out of sixty-six days advertised, they have been stopped by frost thirteen days. On the whole—being out fifty-three days—they have killed thirty-one and a half brace of foxes, ran eleven and a half brace to ground, and had one blank day. There has been no scarcity of foxes till late on in the season, when some of their best coverts were drawn blank; but as the owner of these coverts is well known to be a staunch preserver of foxes, it must have been more bad luck than anything else, as, in shooting the coverts, they have never missed seeing two or three foxes at least. A special word of praise is due to Mr. John Graham, the tenant of the Drums shooting, whose coverts have never been drawn blank. Old Squires keeps as fresh as ever, and his "cheery" voice has lost none of its music. I believe he intends going on another season, and I only hope to see him looking as well at the covert side with his beauties next year. Little George, the first whip, is as active as a kitten, and has been doing very well, but I am sorry to hear he is leaving. The Colonel's hounds have been in splendid form, and with anything like a scent, no fox has been able to live before them. We must now hang up the "old red rag" and betake ourselves to other sports for a while, only hoping that when winter comes round again the same old jovial faces may be spared to meet us at the covert side.

CLYDESDALE BEAGLES.

It has long been felt that a pack of foot beagles would afford excellent sport and a recreative amusement to a number of young men in Glasgow who are fond of hunting, but from business ties can only get away for a half-holiday, and who cannot afford time to ride with fox-hounds. A movement was set on foot some time ago to organize such a pack, and after having been met with the greatest kindness by most of the landed proprietors in the neighbourhood of Glasgow, granting permission to hunt over their lands, eight couple of the Honeywood breed of beagles were purchased at a moderate figure, and arrived about a fortnight ago, averaging about fourteen inches. Among the list of subscribers are the names of many of our best young athletes, a number of whom have shown prominently in most of the local games, such as football, cricket, running, &c., &c. Mr. Robertson Reid, of Gallowflat, has kindly undertaken the duties of Master, and his son, Mr. J. R. Reid, has been appointed secretary. The best thanks of the subscribers are due to the last-named gentleman for the great trouble he has taken in using his best endeavours, assisted by the committee, in getting up the pack. On Saturday the opening meet took place, about the worst day I ever saw; but about 1.30 some of the right sort arrived at Gallowflat, in a well-appointed four-in-hand, a smart tandem following. After partaking of the Master's hospitality, a move was made to Burnside Loch, near which they were not long in finding puss, who gave them a short ringing spurt up to a bit of plantation near Cathkin House. Here the hare had a narrow escape, as Juryman had a snatch at her when breaking covert, but she got away up the hill and was lost. That genuine sportsman and farmer, Mr. Love, of Mid Farm, here invited all present to come in and have "one;" and I can tell you we required it, being wet through, and running all the time knee-deep. Mr. Love finding us another hare, we had another spin, but shortly gave it up, it being such an awful day. I think it right to mention the names of those who had the pluck to come, viz.:—The Master, Mr. J. Reid, Mr. J. R. Reid, Messrs. Scott, Brown (2), Burrell, Smith, Stow, Davie, Whyte, and Buchanan; Major Maclean, Rifle Brigade; Campbell, and "Stringhalt." I forgot to mention that Peter Brown, who whipped-in for some time to the Ayrshire Harriers under Mr. Ewen, has been appointed huntsman, and is giving satisfaction so far. The meets are strictly private, no one is allowed on horseback, and members are admitted only by ballot. A word of **advice to** some gentlemen who run jealous—Don't get *before* the "little dawgs." I have no doubt if we have a fine day next meet there will be a **large turn-out, and I** hope to see some of the fair sex out, **who, I am** sure, **will** enjoy the sport, patronizing us with their smiles.

CLYDESDALE BEAGLES.

I am happy to say this little pack is turning out a great success, and showing capital sport under the able mastership of Mr. R. Reid of Gallowflat. Peter **the** huntsman is doing well, is **a** "beggar" to run, and, like all **Irishmen, is always** full of fun. The ladies are beginning **to take a great interest** in the hunt, **and have turned out** on several occasions **to see** the sport. Every occasion on which they have **been out they** have had great **sport, and as** much running as the keenest would wish. I had an opportunity of seeing their working on Wednesday, and was highly pleased, although they were hunting **under great disadvantages, as the hares were** far too "often." However, the little dogs did well, and were rewarded after a good **spin with blood. It was** amusing to see Peter's face **trying to give a "Who'-hoop"** without any breath! as he had **been running about five miles across** ploughed fields. It should **be borne in mind by those** who criticize the pack, that it has been quickly got up, **is only in** its infancy, and next year there is no doubt the hunt **will** be extremely popular; and I can only advise those young **men who** are fond of a spin across country, coupled with a bit of hunting, to join at once. Mr. J. K. Browne informs **me that** the Garscube day **was** the hardest he has had—so much plough—and I must say I have seldom seen any man go so well over such a severe running country, and often undergoing the extra work of turning the hounds. The thanks of the club are due to the landed proprietors who have kindly given them leave to hunt over their lands; and in every instance, I am happy to say, they have been met with the greatest cordiality by the farmers, without whose good wishes and support there would be no hunting anywhere.

GLASGOW ACADEMICAL CLUB.

This Club finished their football season with a hounds-and-hare run on Saturday. The Meet was at Bearsden, and was graced by a good turn-out of ladies. The hares—Messrs. W. S. Smith and D. H. Watson, of mile-running fame—went off at 3.17, and ten minutes later were followed by the pack of fourteen hounds—the right division, under the lead of Mr. J. W. Arthur, the left under Mr. W. D. Strachan. The day was beautiful, the going good, and everything in favour of a successful run. After leaving Bearsden, the scent lay over Castlehill, which, notwithstanding the opposition of a stalwart "farmer's boy," was safely reached by the whole pack. Here the first check took place, owing to a false scent; but soon the right trail was hit, and the whole went tearing down the hill to the west, the master "coming a cropper" in the first plough. Off they went straight for Duntocher, but after a ten minutes' spin the scent lay back, and it looked as if the hares were making for home, which, however, was a long way off. Another false trail at a farm-house threw the bulk of the pack very badly out, and, though they "harked back," they did not hit it off. Two of the junior division—Messrs. Tod and A. Arthur—had, however, struck the right scent. Soon on the line passing down in front of Garscadden at a good pace the railway was crossed, and all looked like going for Yoker; but, coming to the canal, they went to the left, and all kept along the water's edge. Reaching the Crow Road,

they returned to the canal, and on they went for Kelvin.
Turning down at Kelvindále, a scent improving, they went by
the Kelvin on to Peartree Well, past the mills and the
nursery, and into Burnbank by Lansdowne Crescent. Here
the umpires were ready, and timed as follows :—The hares
arrived at 4.36, being one hour nineteen minutes from time
of starting, neither gentlemen appearing much exhausted.
The first of the hounds put in an appearance fifteen minutes
later, Messrs. Gartley and J. W. Arthur arriving at the head
of the pack within a few seconds of each other; three minutes
later Mr. G. Heron appeared, and then Messrs. A. T. Arthur,
W. D. Strachan, W. S. Heron, A. Tod, Allan Arthur, and W.
Chrystal, in the order named. The hares, as will be seen,
won over the first hounds by five minutes, thus proving their
well-known going qualities. The run was about nine miles,
and was done in seventy-nine minutes. Of the hounds,
Messrs. Gartley, Arthur, Heron, and Strachan ran well; while
Messrs. Buchanan, Chrystal, Taylor, and Tod went a good
course as long as they were in.

OPENING DAY WITH THE LANARKSHIRE AND RENFREWSHIRE FOX-HOUNDS.

" Say, what is wealth without delight?
'Tis dross, 'tis dirt, 'tis useless quite;
Better be poor and taste of joy,
Than thus your wasted time employ.
Then let a humble son of song
Repeat those pleasures most divine;
The joys that life's best hours prolong,
Are those of hunting, love, and wine."

Houston, Saturday, Nov. 1, 1873.—"The first day of the
season!" What emotions of joy do these magic words excite
in the heart of any true sportsman. I can see him taking the
old "red rag" out of the drawer where it has lain, well
peppered, since last season, cogitating over the many good

runs it has seen, and thinking whether it will do another year. " No," he says, " too many bog stains; I have made a good spec. in 'pigs' this year, and I will have a new one." M'Ewen accordingly " suffers." There is no doubt hunting has been from time immemorial the king of sports, but I have no patience with those who run down other sports because they don't care about participating in them. A true sportsman can enjoy every pastime in its season in moderation, without neglecting the duties of that situation in which it has pleased God to place him. Before proceeding to the business part of my article, there is one question I have often been asked, " How is it you can see anything of the sport on foot?" I can only answer that any one who knows the country, and is acquainted with the run of foxes, sometimes sees more on foot than those on horseback (although the latter is preferable). There are plenty of excellent *coin de vantage* in Renfrewshire, from whence you can see a panorama of the whole chase, very often the hounds coming close to you. For instance, any of the hills above Finlayston, the Fereneze Hills, the Pad, &c., &c., not taking into consideration the magnificent views to be had from all these points. I shall be happy to pilot any lover of sport who *can* do his twenty miles a day (he may not have to walk five) any day there is a good meet, and I will guarantee him plenty of sport, a good appetite, and a sound sleep. I may mention that in all my wanderings I have always experienced the greatest kindness from the farmers, and whenever there was a " wee drappie " in the bottle it was never long in making its appearance! Owing to an unaccountable scarcity of foxes in their best cub-hunting country, Squires has not had such a good opportunity of schooling his hounds as in former years; but, with their extraordinary " dash," it is wonderful how he has managed to " steady " them so well. Notwithstanding unfortuitous circumstances, he has brought six brace of cubs to hand with one or two very good spins. In the Lanarkshire county, at Medrox Gorse, thanks to the laird, who is a genuine sportsman and a keen preserver of foxes, they found at once, and went away over very much the same line as they did a year ago, ran to ground, and bolted him; but a tremendous storm coming on, they were obliged to give it up. A run which has hardly been equalled took place while out hunting at Shelford Toll. After finding a good litter in Loch Libo, an old dog fox broke away down towards Uplaw Muir, it being impossible to stop them. Leaving Knockinae to the right, he then turned south, and leaving the Moines Farm to the left, tried the Quarry Mines near the Grange Wood; but not finding any refuge here, he swung to the left round the south side of the Dod Hill, and going over Middleton Muir, came back over the Craig of Carnock, and going straight down to Pollok Castle, they ran into him in the open. Owing to wire, Squires could not get to his hounds during most part of the run. I have seldom heard of a better line of country in olden days, now cursed by wire, than the line the hounds took. Squires has thirty-two and a-half couple of working hounds, including seven couple of young 'uns. Every hound in the kennel has been bred by himself, with the exception of a stallion hound from the York and Ainsty. I never experienced a more inauspicious opening day; it did not only rain, but it deluged, never during the day clearing off for one minute. It being a fine morning to start with, one of the largest fields I have ever seen turned out to show their appreciation of the noble science. I was delighted to see a number of "dear creatures" on side saddles, who, notwithstanding the inclemency of the weather, came gallantly to the front, and I must not forget to mention that a number of ladies, although on four wheels, took an equal interest in the performances of certain gentlemen, with palpitating hearts, when they were going at an extra big wall. I am sorry I cannot lay before your readers a fanciful account of the opening day, as I have really nothing to write about. A brace of foxes were found in Botherwickfield—one went to ground, the other went over the Wreas Road and down to Clives. Slipping out at the south side, he ran down to Houston Wood, and I think crossed into Craigends; but as the Colonel did not wish to disturb these coverts, a move was made for the high country. Found at once in Lawfield Gorse, rattled him twice round the covert, when he broke to the right, on to the Kilmalcolm Strips, where they killed as bad a fox as ever faced the open. It was a very short spin, but young Mr. Ward, nephew of our popular secretary of the Hunt, went well, and was presented with the brush. Found again in Auchenbothie Gorse, and ran up to the strips, but a perfect storm of hail coming on, Squires thought it was no use persevering. During my experience of twenty-five years' hunting, off and on, with these hounds, I have never been out on a worse day, which is saying a good deal. Squires seems to be in as good form as ever; his cheery voice has lost none of its charm, and seems to be quite as clear as when he used to make the Hampshire woods echo "over and over again" with his musical " view hollo !"

A DAY WITH MAJOR HAZELRIGG'S BEAGLES.

Having received a kind invitation to have a day with the Major's "little dawgs," I found myself at Ralston, near Glasgow, on Wednesday week, at two o'clock; and I must say, seldom have I experienced a better day's sport, not even with harriers. A good hare jumped up on the south side of the hill, near the canal, and away they went in view down to the mansion-house and up to the Water Tower. Turning to the right, the hare went back to the field, where she was found, and then ran through the policies. Going round the back of the garden, she lay down in a large stubble field, but went away whenever she heard her enemies, over the Paisley Road at Barshaw, near Alton Farm-house. Going down the hollow, they ran back over the road, and both hare and hounds swam the canal, and ran up to Hillhead Farm-house. From that point she ran down to the canal, then back up the hill and down the hollow. Turning sharp to the left, she jumped up in view, and was raced down to the Cart and back to Main's

Farm, where she was fairly run into, after one hour's hunting. The scent was rather catching, and of course there were a few checks; but the little dogs stuck to their hare well all throughout the run, and it was beautiful to see how they spread at a cast, every one trying for himself. The Master and Mr. J. Kay Brown stuck to them all through the run, and the "Laird" went well during part of it. The field was graced by a number of ladies, who had an excellent view of the run from a knoll at the back of Ralston House. The pack has been out nine times, and killed five hares.

LANARKSHIRE AND RENFREWSHIRE FOX-HOUNDS.

"We will, fair queen, up to the mountain's top,
And mark the musical confusion
Of hounds and echo in conjunction."

Saturday, Nov. 8th, 1873.—Met at Drums, and had a day's sport which has hardly been equalled. After partaking of the hospitality of the tenant, a move was made for the high wood, which, however, was blank, as well as Park Erskine Glen. Both these coverts were exposed to a keen north-eastern wind, and, as it turned out afterwards, the foxes were all lying on the lee side of the hill. Found in West Ferry. The fox broke at the east end, and, crossing the old Greenock Road, went on to Castlehill. Turning sharp back, he then crossed through by Ravenshaw, went up the west corner of Barscube Hill, through the Gleddoch, and swinging round by Barscube Farm-house, ran down to Drums, where they lost him. This was a straggling sort of a run, and the scent catching. In the afternoon they had a "clipper;" in fact, I will be very much mistaken if it will not turn out to be the run of the season. Found in a small patch of gorse on the muir near the west end of Barscube Hill. Before the hounds were half through the whins their sterns began to move. "A fox, for a hundred," says Squires; "have at him, my beauties!" and immediately the Colonel's "view hollo" was heard, "Hoick forrard, away!" and then

> "Such a noise arose
> As the shrouds make at sea in a stiff tempest,
> As loud and to as many tunes."

Away they went, as fast a pack of hounds as any in Scotland—a number of riders finding them a great deal too fast—down over the road and round by the Finlayston side of Knockmountain. Coming back through the above-named covert, he went down the hollow, leaving the strips to the right, and crossed the Dargavel Burn. Here a nasty bit of bog stopped a lot of them, as the hounds were racing. Going up the hill his line then lay by Muirtown, and on into Elphinstone. In a few seconds on swept the musical pack, realizing Somerville's beautiful description :—

> "Hark! from yon covert, where those towering oaks
> Above the humble copse aspiring rise,
> What glorious triumphs burst in every gale
> Upon our ravished ears? The hunter's shout,
> The clanging horns swell their sweet winding notes,
> The pack, wide opening, load the trembling air
> With various melody; from tree to tree
> The propagated cry redoubling bounds,
> And winged zephyrs waft the floating joy
> Through all the regions near,
> The puzzling pack unravel, wile by wile,
> Maze within maze."

Going through Lawfield Gorse, the fox ran over High Barlogan, skirting West Barlogan, and leaving the Scarth to the left, crossed the railway, pointing for Duchal. Going over the Gryffe, he then swung round to the left, and was run to ground at Carruth. Time, forty-five minutes, with only one check at Knockmountain. The pace was tremendous, and only those who got well over the bog were near the hounds, till they caught them at Elphinstone. The gallant Master getting away well, there is no doubt had the best of it all through. Mr. Wallace, dentist, was not far off him; and old

Squires was always there when wanted. Great was the "tailing," and more than one gentleman's horse lay down "clean pumped." After refreshing at Bishopton Inn, the liquor tasting doubly sweet from being supplied to us by the bonnie Miss Mackenzie, the landlady's daughter, we arrived in Glasgow, after a very hard day, about six o'clock. I am happy to say, so far as hunting has gone, the country seems to be very well stocked with foxes.

LANARKSHIRE AND RENFREWSHIRE FOX-HOUNDS.

"The wife around her husband throws
Her arms to make him stay;
'My dear, it rains, it hails, it blows,
You cannot hunt to-day.'
Yet a hunting we will go."
H. Fielding.

Castlesemple, 22nd November.—And it was a bad night, enough to make any man consider twice whether he should send his horse on. But the fates were propitious; although it blew hard, the day turned out well, and scent was good. Drew Greenside and Lawmarnock blank. Found a litter in Shillingworth Gorse; an old fox broke to the right, and went on to Lawmarnock. In the meantime Squires had a cub before him, and hunted him out at the north end, and killed. The fox that broke up the hill went through Lawmarnock, turned to the right over the Locher water, and ran on to the Barcraig (better known as M'Call's Covert), going through which he went by Barmuffloch dam, and on to the Torr. Sinking the hollow, he crossed the Gryffe, and ran through the Scarth to ground at Bortherwickfield. Time, forty-five minutes; but owing to the hounds dividing, it was an unsatisfactory run for the field, and the country they went across frightfully heavy going, although the hounds raced their fox

all the way. With the run-fox a gentleman with a black
coat, Mr. Wallace, and Mr. Couper, had about the best of it
up to the Torr. After crossing the river, Major Hazelrigg, who
had lost a shoe, knicked in, and was **not to** be caught till they
ran to ground. Owing to the heavy going several casualties
occurred, but I am happy to say nobody was hurt.

> " Hunting gives us jocund health,
> We envy not the miser's wealth;
> But chase the fox or timid hare,
> And know delight he cannot share.
> Then home at eve we cheer'ly go,
> While round us brightest comforts shine;
> With joy shut in we shut out woe,
> And sing of hunting, love, and wine!"

LANARKSHIRE AND RENFREWSHIRE FOX-HOUNDS.

> " What conduces to health deserves recommendation,
> 'Twill entail a strong race on the next generation;
> And of all the field games ever practised or known,
> That hunting stands foremost each Briton must own."

Tuesday, 25th.—Met at the Rouken, **found at once, and**
after ringing once or twice round the **covert, he was** run to
ground at Eastwood. Came back, found again, and ran past
Greenback to ground at Williamwood, dug out and killed.

Saturday, 29th.—Craigends, when, **as far** as they have gone,
the run of the season took place. **Found** an old dog-fox in
Houston Wood; went away at once over the Houston Road,
and through Craigends policies. **Not** hanging for **a** moment,
the fox then turned to the right, crossed the **road,** went on
over the Johnstone and Bridge of **Weir** Road, and, leaving
Milliken to the left, ran up the hill to Shillingworth Gorse.
From this point the line lay to the north of the Bar Craig,
and straight on **to** East Torr, where they ran into him.

Time, fifty minutes, with hardly what you would call a check. Squires says this was one of the best runs he has had in this country, and most of the field being with 'em, thoroughly enjoyed it, as it was a case of genuine riding to hounds, seeing them working, and not steeple-chasing after tail hounds. Old Squires went better than ever, and most of the "right sort" were in their usual places.

> "To live a life free from gout, pain, or phthisic,
>   Athletic employment is found the best physic;
>   The nerves are by exercise harden'd and strengthen'd,
>   And vigour attends it by which life is lengthen'd."

CLYDESDALE BEAGLES.

> " Fond echo seems to like the sport,
>   And join the jovial cry;
>   The woods, the hills, the sound retort,
>   And music fills the sky,
>   Then a hunting we will go."
>   *Fielding.*

Saturday, 29th November.—Met at Newton Mearns. Drew the whins at Crosslee Bridge and found immediately. The hare, going away straight to Greenhaggs Hill, went by Netherplace and Malletsheugh. Here the pack divided, but two couple and a-half of the leading hounds stuck to the hunted hare, and pushed her up to the top of Greenhaggs, where she squatted. A check took place, but the hare was viewed doubling back to Malletsheugh, and then, circling away to the left, she went by Kilmuir Dam. By this time Peter, who had been away with another hare, joined in. Puss then went over part of the Mearns Moor, and going over the Kilmarnock Road, crossed the Crook Moss and circled round Hazelden Hill three times. A drenching rain beginning to fall did not improve scent, and after running down to Southfield Wood, on to the left by Westfield and Crook, owing to darkness we were obliged to whip off, after running three hours. The little dogs worked well all through, and never required casting, and

it will be a long time before they see such a run again.
Luckily the honorary secretary got on with the hounds, and,
knowing them, they worked well to him. I am glad to hear
this little pack, which deserves every encouragement, is re-
ceiving much support from the landed proprietors, and is
turning out a great success.

LANARKSHIRE AND RENFREWSHIRE FOX-HOUNDS.

> " See how the morning opes her golden gates,
>   And takes her farewell of the glorious sun!
>   How well resembles it the prime of youth,
>   Trimm'd like a younker, prancing to his love!"

It was one of the finest November mornings when I found
my way, on Saturday last, to Barrochan, to meet the Lanarkshire and Renfrewshire Fox-hounds. Being a favourite meet,
it is unnecessary to say there was a large turn-out of the
patrons of the noble science, both male and female; and I
was pleased to see the "Druid" on "wheels," although he
expressed to me afterwards an opinion that it would have
been better if he had left the horse at home! It is almost
needless for me to reiterate my old remark, that wherever
Scott is keeper foxes are abundant; and as long as the pro-
prietor is Mr. Cunninghame of Craigends, everything is sure
to go straight, being one of the right sort. When the hounds
were thrown into the covert not a sound was heard; but to
anyone conversant with the sport, from the movement of their
sterns, it could easily be seen they were on a drag, as when
they drew up to the earths five cubs and an old 'un jumped up.
All of a sudden it was hollo! here, and hollo! there, enough to
puzzle any hounds; however, as good luck would have it, half
the pack went away with the old 'un, ran him up to Park
Erskine Glen, over Barmore, and down to West Ferry to

ground. Another fox went away from the woods, but as the Colonel wanted to draw the Houston country, he was not persevered with. Found again in the Clives, and ran down nearly to Houston Wood, where, being headed, he turned back and was "worried." Chopped in the Wreas and in Corslie Covert, thus finishing a most unsatisfactory day, and I might almost call it cub-hunting. While I am writing it looks very like that we will have—

> " An envious, sneaking frost,
>   That bites the first-born infants of the spring."

But there is a time for all things. Many a keen fox-hunter is also a curler, and likes to knock over a woodcock now and then, when he gets a chance, in frosty weather.

LANARKSHIRE AND RENFREWSHIRE FOX-HOUNDS.

> "Let the man who's disturbed by misfortune and care
>   Away to the woodlands and valleys repair;
>   Let him hear but the notes of the sweet swelling horn,
>   With the hounds in full cry, and his troubles are gone."

Tuesday, December 2 (Johnstone Castle).—Found at once an old dog-fox, ran him over the Rocks and killed. Found again in the Skifflat. The fox slipped away out at the top end of the covert and made a ring round to Loch Libo; nobody with them. When Squires got up some of the hounds came out of a small strip of plantation with their muzzles bloody, so he thinks they killed. Found again in Bardrain Wood. Went down straight to Johnstone Castle, and killed. Another brace of foxes went to ground.

Saturday, 6th December (Duchal).—Found, and ran up over the moor, and lost. Owing to wire, the field saw nothing of it; back to Duchal, and went away from the

young covert, but lost him near Lawfield. In the meantime a fox had been viewed away from the Kilmalcolm
Strips, and Squires, who was then drawing Auchenbothie
Gorse, quickly got his hounds on the line, and they ran him
down the hollow and over the side of Barscube Hill, but could
not make much of it, owing to roedeer. Went back to
Knockmountain, and found at once in the top end of the
gorse. He broke in view of the field, and running down as if
his point was Finlayston, turned up to the right, and, going
through Park Erskine Glen, went by Corslie Covert on to the
Wreas, where a thick mist coming on they were obliged to
give it up. Time, thirty-five minutes, and a good hunting run.
Col. Buchanan informs me a curious incident happened at the
Shelford Toll meet. Missing two couple of hounds, a labourer
told the Colonel he had seen them "howking" at a hole.
Squires went down, found they had actually dug their fox out
and killed him, as he found the "corpse" at the burrow.

LANARKSHIRE AND RENFREWSHIRE FOX-
HOUNDS.

" If e'er you are plagued with a termagant wife,
  Who, instead of the joy, is the plague of your life, Tally-ho!
  When Madam her small talk begins to let go,
  Then pull on your boots and away, Tally-ho!"

Saturday, January 3, 1874.—Met at Broadfield. I am
happy to say the New Year has opened with a fair day's
sport, and the prospects for the rest of the season are
good. Foxes are plentiful in most parts of our country,
and the keepers, with one exception, are fulfilling the orders
of their masters—namely, to show both game and foxes. A
fox jumped up out of a patch of gorse near Craigmarlock, and
they ran him up to Auchenbothie, where another was on foot,

and the hounds divided, four couple going away towards Duchal. Squires stuck to his hunted fox, and took him up past the Doctor's house on to the Kilmalcolm Strips. He then turned sharp to the right, and crossed the Killalan Road. The hounds here rather got the best of them.

> "Now the fences made skirters look blue,
>   There was no time to crane or to creep,
> O'er the pastures like pigeons they flew,
>   And the ground rode infernally deep.
> Oh! my eyes, what a fall! are you hurt?
>   No, no, sir, I thank you, are you?
> But who, to enjoy such a spirt,
>   Would be grudging an odd rib or two."

On they went a burster, the Colonel taking the left side of the water, Mr. C. Couper, Mr. D. Kippen, Mr. Wallace, and Mr. Clapperton, being well with them, choosing the other side. They raced their fox up to Lawfield Gorse, and, leaving it on the right, went on to Ennely. A thick mist now came on, but Mr. D. Kippen viewed the fox away, and Squires hollo'd the hounds on. They then ran him down the Scarth and up to West Barlogan, where he was viewed dead beat, but owing to another shower of snow, he lived to "fight another day." Time, forty-five minutes, with one check. Trotted back to Auchenbothie, found at once, and had a ring round by the strips.

> "Now the stragglers came in one by one,
>   Hollo! where, my dear fellow, were you;
> Bad luck, in the midst of the run
>   My poor little mare threw her shoe?
> But where was the 'gemman' in pink!
>   Who swore at his tail we should look,
> Not in the next parish, I think,
>   For he never got over the brook."

A VISIT TO LORD EGLINTON'S KENNELS.

" My hounds are bred out of the Spartan kind,
So strong, so sanded ; and their heads are hung
With ears that sweep away the morning dew ;
Crook-kneed and dew-lapped, like Thessalian bulls ;
Slow in pursuit, but matched in mouth like bells,
Each under each. A cry more tuneable
Was never hollo'd to, nor cheer'd with horn."

Shakespeare.

I can hear Cox saying, Shakespeare must have been a humbug, and no judge of hounds, as my hounds are neither "crook-kneed" nor slow in pursuit, as, with a good scent, nobody can catch 'em ; but the above lines by the immortal bard show he must have been a sportsman, and those who have read his works must have seen that, whenever he had an appropriate occasion, he always extolled the noble science of hunting. By the kind permission of his lordship I had an opportunity, at what might almost be called the beginning of the season, of visiting his kennels. After partaking of Mrs. Cox's hospitality, and having a talk with Cox about that "inexplicable" subject, scent, he introduced me to the young entry, and a better set of young 'uns I have seldom, if ever, seen. Beginning at the top of the tree, his lordship breeds a good deal from Furrier. This stallion hound is by the Hon. G. Fitzwilliam's Fencer out of Lord Eglinton's Mischief. Mischief was by Sir R. Sutton's Bagazet. This hound, along with Gambler, a three-year-old by Furrier out of Gossamer ; Lincoln, a black and tan, very nice hound, by Lord Poltimore's Labourer out of Fallacy ; and Castor by the Hon. G. Fitzwilliam's Bentinck out of Lord Eglinton's Carnage, were the four hounds that gained the cup at Harrowgate. It is curious to note that Carnage was one of the last hounds sold at old Tattersall's yard at Villebois' sale. Cox has another cup over his mantlepiece, which he gained at Malton with Flourish out of Fancy, and Gaiety by Furrier out of Gossamer. I must now hark back to the young 'uns ; and looking over Cox's beauties, I found the cream of the entry were Furrier's. He began with sixteen couple, and politeness induces sportsmen always to give the ladies the preference. We will give the names of the cream of 'em:—Dewdrop by Dexter out of Gossamer, Legacy by Leveller out of Rarity, Malady by Driver out of Milliner, and Racket and Rally by Furrier out of Ruby. Worth going five hundred miles to see. Next come the dogs:—Duster by Dexter out of Gossamer, Factor by Furrier out of Frolic, Lucifer by Lord Poltimore's Roman out of Lively. Roman was one of the three couple that was sold at Lord Poltimore's sale, and purchased for £600 by Major Brown. Racer, Random, and Ringwood, by Flyer out of Reckless. With regard to the old hunting entry, I will reserve my account for another edition of your paper. During the cub-hunting season the scent has been bad; but hunting six days a-week, Cox has added thirty-nine brace of noses to the kennel door. They have had one or two good day's sport since the stubble was cleared. The last day's cub-hunting the dog pack found a litter of cubs in the Dean's, had forty minutes, and killed. Took another cub away, and ran into him in twenty-five minutes. Found an old dog fox up the Crawfordland Water. Went away to Grass Mill, and on over a splendid country to Tour, leaving Kilmaurs on the left, to Stewarton, where they ran into him in the open—a fast twenty-five minutes.

Cassillis, Friday, Nov. 7th (Dog pack).—Drew Blairbowie and Main's Wood blank, but found near Boreland Glen. Went away, leaving Skeldon House on the right by Venston to Torr Hill, then leaving Guiltriehill Wood on the right he was run to ground at Millsmuir Glen—a brilliant forty-five minutes. The Marquis of Ailsa, Lady Julia Follet and her sister, Mr. Oswald, Mr. W. Baird, Captain Hay Newton, Mr. Ewen, and the Laird of Guiltriehill went well throughout.

Nov. 10.—Met at Aiket Castle. Bitch pack: found at Lainshaw; he faced the open in the direction of Busby, and leaving Kilmaurs Mains on the right, went by Langside to

Crosshill, and was run to ground near Kilmaurs Village.
Found again at Kilmaurs Covert; had a very fast twenty
minutes and killed in the open.

Nov. 25.—Dog pack: met at Barskimming; had twenty-five
minutes to ground. Found again, had a clipping forty
minutes, and a kill in the open.

Nov. 27 (Sundrum).—Dog pack: had a first rate thirty
minutes, and killed at Martnaham.

Foxes are plentiful in most parts of the country, but I am
sorry to say in the Aiket Castle and Dunlop country vulpecidism prevails. Bill Brackenboro' still continues as first
whip, and I am happy to say his *cara sposa* has pretty well
recovered from her accident. Andrews, Cox tells me, is still
in his old form—one of the best kennel men in the world;
and with everything *couleur de rose*, I hope that it may be
my privilege to write some further accounts of sport with his
lordship's pack.

CLYDESDALE BEAGLES.

> " Ye fox-hunters, stag, ay, and hare-hunters too,
> Whose aim is to rub off the furrows of care,
> Like Nimrods the fleet-footed pussy pursue,
> And taste of the sweets of the morn-breathing air!"

1874.—Yesterday, a joint meet of the Clydesdale and
Major Hazelrigg's Beagles took place. It being a rare thing
in this country for two packs to hunt together, a good deal of
curiosity was excited to see how they would work; but I am
sorry to say there was a very poor turn-out to witness this
capital day's sport. However, those who were there were of
the rare good sort, and a very good run took place, although
from the frightful state of the country the late Charley West-
hall could not have lived with him. Found at once near
Darnley Mains, and went away over the road towards the
railway, where a number of hounds flashed on to the high
wood near Kinnishead. Peter, the Clydesdale huntsman,

went on to try and stop them. The Major, who had the horn, stuck to his hunted hare, and ran her back down by Darnley Toll, past the mill, and up over the hill, round again by Darnley Mains to the Busby Road, where she made a somersault into the road. The Major here cast forward, but the hare had doubled behind him. They picked it up with a catching scent, and ran over the old Barrhead Road, past Leggatstone Farm-house, down to the Brock Water. Here a well-known athlete, of the "Clydesdale Beagles," boldly went at the flooded water, and, after a ducking, got well over. If they had picked it up at once, he would have been the only man with them, the rest of the field getting over by the broken branch of a tree. There was a little slow hunting afterwards, but as it was evident pussy had saved herself in the Pollok Woods, and Peter turning up with the rest of the hounds, the Major tried again. In a ploughed field on the north side of the old Darnley Toll Road another hare jumped up, and they ran her straight as an arrow over the Busby Road, and nearly on to Patterton, but a tremendous rainstorm coming on, the hounds were stopped. The first run would be about an hour and a half, of course a good deal of ringing; the second fifteen minutes. I never, in all my experience of running with beagles, saw the country in such a state, and the next time I go out I think I shall hire a "boat."

EXTRAORDINARY LONG RUN WITH THE LANARKSHIRE AND RENFREWSHIRE FOX-HOUNDS.

> "This bleak and frosty morning,
> All thoughts of danger scorning,
> Our spirits brightly flow—
> We're all in a glow,
> Through the sparkling snow
> While a-hunting we go,
> To the sound of the merry horn."

Bridge of Weir, Saturday, January 17, 1874.—In this

extraordinary climate it is impossible to know what change of weather will take place in twelve hours. I went to bed on Friday night, when it was pouring, and when I awoke next morning I saw a boy sliding on the pavement, and "didn't I hate that boy." However, the report was that it "would do," and down we went to the Meet, luckily to witness one of the greatest runs that has ever taken place in our country. Drew the Torr blank, trotted away to the Bar Craig and found at once; ran him up to the end of the covert, where, being headed by a number of people on foot (who, in spite of warning, will surround the coverts, and spoil their own sport), he turned back underneath the rocks, and the "Druid" and myself viewed him away with the hounds at his brush, and not a soul near them—the field all being on the other side of the wood. Although there was a sprinkling of snow on the ground, scent was breast-high, and they raced him across the boggy hollow up to the Torr Wood, going through which he ran down by Torr House, then wheeled to the right and crossed the Gryfe. Some of the field here got up, most of whom went over the bridge round by the Bridge of Weir, a few fording the river. The fox then went round the west end of the Scarth and up towards West Barlogan (here the field first got a view of the hounds far ahead); turning to the right, he left Ennely to the left, and went on by Botherwick-field down to Clives, which he did not enter, ran straight on to Houston Wood. The only men who were up at Clives were Squires, and Messrs. E. Collins, Holms, and J. Buchanan. Crossing the road, they ran on to Craigends, where a good deal of time was lost ringing the coverts; however, eventually he broke back over the road, and going as straight as an arrow through Houston Wood, up again he went, through the Clives this time, and on by the Wreas and Elphinstone, over Ennely, down to the Scarth. This gallant fox did not hang here, but went right through the wood and down to the Gryfe, evidently making for his old quarters. Most of the field again went round by the road. A farmer having informed a well-known member of the Hunt that the river was quite fordable, he piloted a number of the field down, but his horse made too big a spring, and, quoting Warburton, slightly altered—

> "In the run, said a sportsman, just as I led,
> My horse jumped in the brook and went bang overhead;
> Like a whale in the water I floundered about,
> And being thrown in, I of course was thrown out."

When he came up, his language to the farmer was anything but "Parliamentary;" but eventually, a kindly *public* being at hand, he got home all right, none the worse for his ducking. After crossing the Gryfe, the hounds ran up again to the Torr, going through which the fox went out over the muir, turned to the right, and saved his brush in a drain at Carruth, and being such a gallant fox, no attempt was made to dig him out. They were going two hours and a half, and must have ran over about eighteen miles of country. In the first part of the run there was no doubt it was catch 'em if you can, with now and then a sight of them; but in the latter part the field were pretty well with them. A good deal of time was put off about Houston Wood; but the hounds were hunting all the time, and although they ran to a point and back again, it was the longest run I have seen in my day. The hounds never were cast, and hunted through this long run admirably. On the way home, a farmer who had witnessed the latter part of the run from the top of a hill, addressed Mr. Matheson as follows:—"Weel, hae ye kilt your fox?" On Mr. M. saying no, he expressed satisfaction, saying—"I ken him weel; ye've hunted that ane for twelve years; they telt me he was shot last year, but I think he'll gie ye another run yet." Tired horses were the order of the day on the ride home, and tremendous were the jumps when some members got their legs under the mahogany, but—

> "To friendship, true friendship the toast shall go round,
> To love and the pleasure derived from the chase;
> For while love and friendship in union are found,
> What bliss can of hunting, fox-hunting, take place."

LANARKSHIRE AND RENFREWSHIRE FOX-HOUNDS.

Houston, Saturday 10th, 1874.—A large field and a great number of carriage people, amongst whom I was glad to see my friend the "Druid" out again on wheels, with a galaxy of beauty on board. Found a leash of foxes in Borthwickfield the moment the hounds were thrown into covert. One broke for Craigends, and one for Clives; but the hounds went away with another down to the Scarth, and swinging round by West Barlogan, went up the Ennely. There the field were a little thrown out. The hounds brought their fox down through the hollow, and Mr. G. Muir and myself, who were on foot, viewed him back into Borthwickfield. The pack here flashed on, and by the time they cast themselves on to the line, Squires and the field got up. They ran through the covert.

> " He then broke away with the hounds at his brush,
> When each gallant sportsman right onward does push ;
> Hark forward, my lads! now, hark forward, away—
> No funking at walls, for we've no time to stay !"

Going out at the south side, the hounds divided, two foxes being on foot. Squires went away with one over a nice bit of country, down across the Bridge of Weir Road on to Crosslee, where they killed him. Trotted back and found the Colonel had run the other fox round by Duchal and up to the Kilmalcolm Strips, where he lost him. Chopped a fox in Elphinstone; but had no more sport. Miss Whitehill went well in this run, and she had a nasty fall, remounted, and was well up at the finish.

Gleniffer, Tuesday, 13th.—Found and ran down to Newton Wood, near Elderslie, pretty sharp, the fox finding refuge in a drain. During this spin a well-known old member of the Hunt, who always goes well, got a nasty cropper. In jumping a wall, riding a first-rate fencer, on landing on the other side his horse put his foot in a grip and rolled over him. I am happy to say that he was able to ride home not much the worse. I observed, however, next day, that he was going a little "short" on the near fore leg. Went back, found in Trees Gorse, and ran down to Gleniffer, again into a drain. It was a frightfully windy, stormy day, and in consequence the sport on the whole was very moderate, and every one—

> " Was glad to go home to the smoking sirloin,
> And cherish his heart with the generous wine;
> To drink in a bumper to each lovely lass,
> And many choice fellows to toast in his glass."

LANARKSHIRE AND RENFREWSHIRE FOX-HOUNDS.

> "For coffee-house gossip some hunters come out,
> Of all matters prating, save that they're about;
> From scandal to cards they to "politics" roam,
> They ride forty miles, head the fox, and go home!
> Such sportsmen as these we good fellows condemn,
> And I vow we'll ne'er drink a 'quæsitum' to them."
>
> *Warburton.*

1874.—What with politics and frost, there has not been much doing in the hunting field lately. One good thing took place from Milliken on a snowy morning, when they ran their fox over the Torr down by Duchal, and back over the Gryfe on to Clives. After this it was impossible to tell where they went, as nobody was with them, and Squires had to go home and get a fresh horse before he got his hounds. I am sorry to say that on Saturday the 7th most of our best country was drawn blank, but late in the afternoon they found a fox in Clives, and ran a short ring round by the Wreas and Scarth to Borthwickfield to ground.

Tuesday.—Stopped by frost.

Saturday, 13th (Bridge of Weir).—A very large field, with a number of fair faces on wheels; but I missed the blooming countenance of my friend the "Druid." Much to the astonishment of every one, the whole coverts were drawn blank, which previously were well stocked with foxes; and over this part of the country some of the best runs of the season have taken place. On a well-known sportsman being asked how he could account for this state of matters, he answered in the following terms:—How could we expect sport, the country has been so overrun lately with Liberal canvassers that all the well-bred foxes have gone to Ayrshire, thus spoiling our sport. However, it is to be hoped that after the turmoil of election is over the "noble animal" will once more return to his "native heath."

> " We hold in abhorrence all vulpecide knaves,
>   With their gins and their traps, and their velveteen slaves;
>   They may feed their fat pheasants, their foxes destroy,
>   And mar the prime sport they themselves can't enjoy;
>   But such sportsmen as these we good fellows condemn,
>   And I vow we'll ne'er drink a ' quæsitum' to them."
>
> *Warburton.*

CLYDESDALE BEAGLES.

Wednesday, 4th.—Met at Tollcross House, where Mr. George Dunlop, one of our most promising young sportsmen, and a chip of the old block, in the absence of his father, dispensed the usual hospitalities. A hare was at once found in a ploughed field near the house, and, after a capital run, although very much of a ring, was ultimately lost. Found again outside the policies, and had a clipping hour and a kill in the open. Peter, young Mr. Dunlop, and a well-known member of the Hunt, who is seldom far away from them, were all there. The little "dawgs" hunted their hare very patiently all through the run, with a very catching scent, and I was glad to see them at last rewarded with a "scut." I have had the pleasure of participating in the sport of this excellent little pack of beagles several times this season, and am

surprised that more young men don't take advantage of this
exhilarating amusement. Saturday is usually a sort of half-
holiday, and the hounds don't generally meet till two o'clock.
The season is now nearly over, but next year I hope to see a
great addition to the rank of subscribers, as a more health-
giving and gentlemanly amusement does not exist.

LANARKSHIRE AND RENFREWSHIRE FOX-HOUNDS.

> "Free from care, from pain, from sorrow,
> Haste to Finlayston to-morrow,
> There shall our steeds outstrip the wind,
> While time and age creep far behind.
> No long vigils of love we keep,
> Nor evening cups protract our sleep;
> But ere the sun has reached the skies,
> Fresh as the morn we gladly rise."

Tuesday, 17th (Neilston Station). — Found at once in
Uplaw Muir. The fox crossed the road and ran up the hill to
Loch Libo Coverts, but wheeled down by the loch, and went
up the steep hill on the north side of the toll, where the horsemen got behind. In getting to the top, the hounds were seen
streaming away over the moss. Here they threw up, and
Squires could not get to them, but they cast beautifully themselves and raced away on to the Skiff, going through which,
at least ten minutes ahead of the field, they ran their fox
down to the strip near Howood Toll. They then rattled
him out of this, and threw up at an old deserted farm-house,
when they feathered all round about. Mr. D. Kippen, who
thought the fox must be somewhere near, jumped off his
horse and poked about with his whip, and sure enough there
was Mr. Foxy snugly hid in an old pigstye, when, it is needless to say, he will never rob another hen-roost. This was a
very fine run for hounds, but from the state of the going it
was impossible to live with them.

N

Saturday, 21st (Finlayston).—A nasty, drizzly morning, and a large field out. After partaking of the hospitality of that prince of sportsmen, Mr. George Kidston, and the "coffee housing" having been got over, a move was made to the East Wood. But much to Hay's disappointment they did not find, as three foxes had been seen in the covert last time they were shooting. However, they found in the gorse at the east; but the field being very unruly, they could make nothing of it. Drew Craigmarlock blank. In the meantime, a fox was viewed away from Knockmountain. Squires quickly got his hounds laid on, and away they went a burster down the hollow and up by Barscube. Leaving it on the left, he crossed the burn and raced on by Corslie to Elphinstone, going through the corner of which he came back very nearly the same line to Knockmountain, where, I think, they must have changed foxes, as I viewed a fresh one come down into the Kilmalcolm Strips with the hounds. I hear they made nothing of it after this. It was to be regretted, as the hounds deserved blood. Time, fifty minutes, with hardly a check. Every one confessed that Mr. D. Kippen, riding a new purchase, had the best of it all through.

> " Oh, hour of bliss !
> To equal this
> Diana strove in vain;
> Thrice happy man,
> Who, 'in the van,'
> His place can well maintain."
>
> *Nimrod.*

> "Near to him, on his gray, who never rides jealous,
> Cramming over his fences came the game Wallace;
> But his neck he must break, surely, sooner or late,
> As he'd rather ride over than open a gate."

Mr. Geo. Dunlop, Mr. Geo. Kidston, Mr. Thorburn (Greenock), Mr. Hunt, Lord Blantyre's head-keeper, Mr. Couper, and Squires went well. Many were the "cripples" after it was all over, especially amongst the young 'uns, and great was the demand for brandy and soda in the excellent little Kilmalcolm Hotel. One word of advice to beginners. When your horse gets **weak** in a run, don't look for **a** gap in a wall (as so many are **apt to** do) where there are lots of loose stones and the ground generally much cut up, but look to where the ground is good to rise from, for without a proper fulcrum **the** exertion of leaping is doubled.

LANARKSHIRE AND RENFREWSHIRE FOX-HOUNDS.

" Oh, give me the man to whom nought comes amiss—
  One horse or another, that country or this;
  Through falls and bad starts who undauntedly still
  Rides up to this motto, 'Be with 'em I will,'
  Quæsitum! Quæsitum! fill up to the brim,
  We'll drink, if we die for't, a bumper to him!"

Warburton.

Saturday, 28th (Bishopton).—A lovely morning, **and a very** large field out. **A move was made** to Barrochan Moss, and in less than a minute a hearty cry pealed through the thick covert—" Tally-ho! gone away!" rung from the lips of the whipper-in, as he viewed the biggest fox *that ever was seen* break away from **the** corner. " Hoick! to, hollo!" cried Squires, in his musical voice. " For'ard! for'ard!"—and every hound answered by bursting **from** the wood. " Hold hard! let them get at it!" cried the Colonel **to** some eager sportsmen. They ran him through Dargavel policies, along the **burn, and** up by the north wood at Barrochan. The field, who were all **waiting** on the road, got to the leading grounds, **but Squires and** the Colonel were thrown out, having taken the wrong side at Dargavel. Going over the top of the hill at Barrochan, he raced down over the road near the mill to Clives, and going through the corner of the wood went **on to** Botherwickfield (all grass). They hung here for about **ten** minutes. Squires having now got up, found his hounds lying at the earth, and he told me he thinks the fox must have scratched himself in under the stopping. In the meantime, a fox was viewed away at the south side, and the hounds, quickly getting on the line, ran him, leaving the Wreas on the right, on to Ennely. Disdaining to enter the Scarth, he kept to the right, over the Knapp's Muir, where it was very nasty going, ran down over the Greenock Road, and, going over the railway, crossed the Gryfe, and went on to a young plantation on the side of the new Duchal avenue. Yard by yard his enemies gained upon him, but still he continued to do his best endeavours to escape. The refreshing hope that an open earth was near revived his drooping spirits, and fagged Reynard redoubled his exertion to gain this haven of security. "You may try, and I like to see you," said old Squires. "It's a brave heart that never flags when misfortune's at the heels." (Some thought that the fox here had run *through* a drain, but this was impossible, as there was a grating at the other end). There is a high built wall runs along here, and the fox, raising his brush, managed to get over it. Many of the hounds fell backwards as they jumped at it; but at last all got over, and they now swept up the hill past the toll, and on by the keeper's house, to a small spinney, when Squires' "Who'-hoop!" was carried far on the breeze. It was poor Reynard's death-knell. Time, one hour and a quarter, including the check at Botherwickfield. With the exception of a bit of road at the finish, they went over a very good country. Up to the drain, Mr. C. T. Couper, Mr. Wallace, and Mr. George Coats were first up. Altogether, this was one of the best hunting runs they have had this year. I was rather amused with the cool way in which some men, after going through a gate, slam it back in other sportsmen's faces.

> " Some riders there are, who, too jealous of place,
>   Will fling back a gate in their next neighbour's face;
>   Never pull up when a friend gets a fall;
>   Some ride over friends, hounds, and horses and all.
>   Such riders as these we good fellows condemn,
>   And I vow we'll ne'er drink a 'quæsitum' to them."
>   *Warburton.*

Found again at once in Elphinstone. He broke at the north side, went a cracker on to Knockmountain and down the hollow. He then came back up the hill and turned sharp to the right down again to Finlayston. A check here took place, and the field, thinking it was all over, went down to partake of Mr. George Kidston's well-known hospitality. Old Squires, however, with his indomitable perseverance, Mr. D. Kippen and the Colonel, keen as ever, determined not to be beat, went on, and they fairly ran into their fox in the open near Broadfield—time, forty minutes—Mr. Kippen getting the brush, thus finishing one of the best *all round* days of the season.

> " With closing daylight, when our pastime ends,
> Together dining, we all part good friends;
> And home returning, we our slumber court.
> Of hounds and hunting, some fresh knowledge then
> Shall guide the quill when 'Stringhalt' writes again!"

SPLENDID HUNTING RUN WITH THE LANARK-SHIRE AND RENFREWSHIRE FOX-HOUNDS.

On Tuesday, the 12th, these hounds met at Crookston Castle, with about forty of a field, and at once found one of the right sort.

The fox broke at the east end of the covert towards Pollok House, and after a sharp hunt past the edge of the policies, he crossed the Barrhead Road, going over the hill through the Pollokhead Wood, and on across the railway, as if his point was Waulkmill Glen; but, changing his mind, he turned to the left over a fine open country, where the pace was all that could be desired. Leaving Patterton Quarry on the right, crossed the Stewarton Road, up a hill to Capelrig. Here he turned sharp to the left, and made for the Rouken Mines, where it was feared he would get to ground; but, though he tried them, he disdained such an ignoble way of saving his brush, and on he went crossing the Kilmarnock Road by Cleuch Farm, to Eastwood Mains, where there was a short check. The hounds soon hit it off again, and hunted him slowly over the hill by Carrolside Farm, crossing both the old Mearns and Eaglesham Roads, down to the Cart, which he swam, a quarter of a mile above Busby Works. The pace again improved here; passed the Dripps and Reel, crossing the Kilbride Road and Kittoch Burn; thence passed the Kittoch Mill, and on to near the Netherton Braes, where he was run into the open within a hundred yards of the breeding earths of Castlemilk. Time, one hour and twenty-five minutes; distance, about eleven miles. The fox having been gone from Crookston ten minutes before the hounds, of course there was some slow hunting and a few checks, with every now and then a brilliant burst; but to any true lover of the noble science, it was a perfect treat to see the patient and persevering manner in which old Squires hunted his fox over a difficult, and, in some places, rough country. This, no doubt, will be one of the best runs of the season, 1867-68.

The brush was presented to Mr. Allan Scott, an old, well-known heavy weight, a staunch supporter of the Hunt.

THE PAST HUNTING SEASON.

"What lengths we pass! Where will the wandering chase
Lead us bewildered? Smooth as swallows skim
The new-shorn mead, and far more swiftly fly.
See the brave pack how to the head they press,
Jostling in close array, then, more diffuse,
Obliquely well, while from their opening vollied mouths
The thunder breaks.

Look back and view
The strange confusion of the vale below,
Where sore vexation reigns.

> Old age laments
> His vigour spent; the tall, plump, brawny youth
> Curses his cumbrous bulk, and envies now
> The short pigmean race, he whilom kenn'd,
> With proud insulting leer. A chosen few
> Alone the sport enjoy, nor droop beneath
> Their pleasing toils."
>
> *Beckford.*

The season is over! and never in the recollection of the oldest sportsmen has it been so open, and have our local pack had so many good runs; and although the country has ridden awfully heavy, there have been comparatively few casualties to men and horses. With the exception of a serious accident to a lady's favourite horse, and the breaking of Mr. M. T. Fozier's collar-bone (Mr. Fozier, I am happy to say, is going on all right), no other serious accidents have occurred. Colonel Buchanan has been out fifty-eight days, and has killed 22½ brace of foxes, stopped by frost two days, three blank days, and one day—the last of the season—was so stormy. Major Hazelrigg, of the 21st Regiment, who keeps a capital pack of beagles, has shown some excellent sport, and has killed eighteen hares, having had one blank day. I think he was out thirty-one times. Mr. J. Addie, who also keeps a private pack and hunts them himself (as also does the Major), has had a capital season, and killed fifteen hares. Mr. Ewen, of Ewenfield, who is Master of the Ayrshire Harriers, has had good sport, and wound up the season with a paper hunt, which came off at the old country near the Wallace Monument, over a stiffish course. There was the usual jealousy at starting, some of the Aryshire men trying hard for a start. Mr. Dykes made the running on old Sunbeam, and was in the front till passing Craigie Castle, closely followed by Mr. C. Cunninghame, Mr. Wallace, and Mr. Cockburn, with Mr. R. Oswald, Mr. W. Baird, and Captain W. Middleton not far off waiting their time. Here at a fence, with a ditch on the take off, Mr. Dykes and Mr. Cunninghame came to grief, and Mr. Wallace took the lead, which he kept till the Craigie Road was crossed, the next being Messrs. Oswald, Middleton, and Baird. Mr. Wallace here loosing the scent, went a little out of the way, but getting on the line again a slashing finish took place, the riders arriving in the following order:—Mr. W. Baird, Mr. Wallace, Captain Middleton, Mr. Oswald, Mr. C. Cunninghame, Mr. Cockburn, and Mr. Dykes. Young Mr. Dick M'Farlane went well throughout. Mr. Cockburn, when going well, was cannoned against near the finish, and fell. The Clydesdale beagles have had some good spins, but have been unfortunate in not bringing many hares to hand, owing a good deal to the boisterous state of the weather, and there being so many hares in a good deal of the country, causing so many changes. They also finished their season with a short steeple-chase at the Mearns Muir, where, I am informed, Mr. John Buchanan had the best of it. I have not heard from Cox, Lord Eglinton's huntsman, but I understand he has killed over eighty brace of foxes. The old coat may now be hung up for the season, and I may put past my favourite pen with which I have had the pleasure of describing so many capital runs this season. As old "Jorrocks" says, "Summer is now drawing on, at least it ought to, if its a comin' at all, leavin' us a long season of repose to contemplate the past and speculate on the future—that uncertain future to which we all look forward with such presumptuous certainty! Oh, my beloved hearers, summer is a dreadful time. Whoever talked of the winter of our discontent talked like an insane man and no sportsman! I knows no more melancholic ceremony than takin' the string out of one's 'at at the end of the season, foldin' hup and puttin' away the old red rag—a rag unlike all other rags, the dearer and more valuable the older and more worthless it becomes." I hardly agree with the celebrated Mr. J., however, as every sport has its season, and can be enjoyed by all true sportsmen.

> " Though midnight her dark frowning mantle is spreading,
> Yet Time flies unheeded where Bacchus resides ;
> Fill, fill, then, your glasses, his power never dreading,
> And drink to the hounds o'er which Buchanan presides.

Though toast after toast with great glee has been given,
  The highest top-sparkling bumper decides
That for stoutness, pace, beauty, on this side of heaven,
  Unrivalled the hounds o'er which Buchanan presides!
    Then drink to the fox-hounds,
      The high-mettled fox-hounds;
  We'll drink to the hounds o'er which Buchanan presides.
      Who'-hoop!"

LIST

OF

THE LANARKSHIRE AND RENFREWSHIRE FOX-HOUNDS.

NOVEMBER, 1873.

AGE.	NAME.	SIRE.	DAM.
8 Years,	Wisdom, ...	Belvoir Striver, ...	Wishful.
	Monitor, ... ⎫ Marmion, .. ⎭	Marplot, ...	Matchless.
7 Years,	Waspish, ...	Challenger, ...	Welcome.
6 Years,	Gratitude, . ⎫ Gossip, ... ⎭	Governor, ...	Wisdom.
	Fountain, ...	Lictor, ...,..........	Welcome.
	Comus, ... ⎫ Charity, ... ⎭	Dexter, ...	Careful.
	Barrister, ...	Grove Barrister, ...	York and Ainsty Gaudy.
5 Years,	Grafton, ...	Wonder, ...	Garland.
	Bertram, ...	Dexter, ...,.........	Bravery.
	Stormer, ...	Wellington, ...	Artful.
	Denmark, .. ⎫ Duster, ... ⎬ Damper, ... ⎭	Tickler, ...	Dorcas.
	Landlord, ...	Limner, ...	Careful.
4 Years,	Conqueror, ⎫ Chorister, .. ⎬ Comfort, ... ⎭	Wellington, ...	Careful.
	Wishful, ... ⎫ Woodbine, ⎬ Welcome, .. ⎭	Lord Poltimore's Lancelot, ...	Wisdom.
	Trimmer, ... ⎫ Twilight, ... ⎬ Tempest, ... ⎭	Lord Fitzhardinge's Warrior, ...	Tempest.

AGE.	NAME.	SIRE.	DAM.
3 Years,	Mimic, ... Mindful, ... Mischief, ...	Marmion, ...	Garland.
	Governess, ...	Governor,.............	Gladsome.
	Whimsey,.....	Tickler,................	Wisdom.
	Driver, ... Dorcas, ... Diligence,..	Marmion, ...	Duchess.
	Rutland, ... Ruby, ...	Dexter, ...	Gertrude.
2 Years,	Hercules, .. Hermit,.... Harpy,......	Fife Hercules,........	Gossip.
	Wrangler,.. Windsor,... Wildare,...	Denmark, ...	Wanton.
	Striver, ... Solon, ...	Lord Fitzhardinge's Desperate,..........	Stately.
	Madcap, ... Magic, ...	Marmion, ...	Wisdom.
2 Years,	Dexter, ... Desperate,.	Lord Fitzhardinge's Desperate, ...	Wary.
	Governor,.. Gamester,.. General,....	Damper, ...	Garland.
1 Year,	Nigel, ... Nimrod, ... Nelson, ... Norman, ... Niobe,......	York and Ainsty Barrister,...........	Garland.
	Trusty, ... Timely, ... Toilet, ...	Damper, ...	Twilight.
	Bellman, ... Bluecap, ...	York and Ainsty Barrister,...........	Wishful.
1 Year,	Richmond,. Riot, ...	York and Ainsty Barrister,...........	Ruby.
	Baronet, ...	York and Ainsty Barrister,...........	Wisdom.
	Gladsome, ...	Denmark,.............	Gratitude.

8 Years old,	...	...		...	3	Hounds.
7 ,,	...	...		...	1	,,
6 ,,	...	...		...	6	,,
5 ,,	...	...		...	7	,,
4 ,,	...	...		...	9	,,
3 ,,	...	...	...	...	10	,,
2 ,,		...	...	...	15	,,
1 ,,	...	...	...	...	14	,,
		Total,	...	...	32½	Couples.

In conclusion, I beg to thank those gentlemen who have many times assisted me in writing accounts of runs, especially Col. Buchanan, Mr. C. T. Couper, Mr. D. Kippen, and the able acting Secretary of the Hunt, Mr. Adam Morrison. I may also mention the great civility all hunting men have always received from the landladies of the Houston and Bishopton Hotels, where, many a time, when soaked through, I have sat down at a roaring fire and had a good hot tumbler. Nor must I forget the wonderful good Scotch broth that Mrs. Money at Bishopton has always ready for any sportsman when the hounds are in that district, tasting all the better by being served by her pretty daughter, Miss Mackenzie.

www.ingramcontent.com/pod-product-compliance
Lightning Source LLC
Chambersburg PA
CBHW030629270326
41927CB00007B/1361